FORAGER'S HARVEST 101

Forager's Harvest 101: A Comprehensive Guide to Identifying, Preserving, and Preparing Wild Edible Plants, Mushrooms, Berries, and Fruits – FULL COLOR Pictures of Every Plant and Delicious Recipes.

Diane Wells

★★★★★

PREPPING WITH WILD FOODS

 SCAN THE QR CODE TO DOWNLOAD IT

WITH THIS BONUS YOU WILL:

Uncover a fresh, diverse, and adaptable prepping approach to ensure you always have access to vital resources, no matter the circumstance.

Learn survivalist cooking techniques to craft nourishing meals from foraged finds, even with limited resources.

Learn how to harness foraged plants to create essential tools like ropes and baskets, enhancing your survival toolkit.

Explore the potential of wild insects as a lifeline during unforeseen disasters, adding a unique dimension to your survival strategy.

Acknowledgments

To those picking up *Forager's Harvest 101*, and to all who walk alongside me on this remarkable journey,

First and foremost, I owe a boundless debt of gratitude to my grandparents in Georgia. In the verdant fields, under the shade of towering trees, and by the humming Creekside, they planted within me a seed of reverence for nature. They taught me not just to observe, but to feel – to sense the heartbeat of the land and to appreciate the stories whispered by the winds. It was in those early days, with dirt under my nails and the scent of wildflowers in the air, that my love for the natural world took root.

This book is not solely a testament to my experiences but also an ode to their wisdom and love. Their spirits have been my guiding light, illuminating my path even in the darkest thickets and most bewildering crossroads.

I also wish to extend my heartfelt thanks to my diligent team, whose unwavering support and expertise transformed a dream into the tangible pages you hold now. To my readers, your curiosity and passion are the very lifeblood of this endeavor. *Forager's Harvest101* is as much yours as it is mine.

Lastly, to nature herself – my eternal muse and teacher. In your embrace, I've found solace, inspiration, and an understanding deeper than words. This book is but a humble offering in gratitude for the lessons and wonders you bestow upon us each day.

May we all continue to grow, learn, and cherish the beautiful world around us.

With profound gratitude,

- Diane Wells

Table of Contents

Chapter 1: Introduction to Foraging.. **11**

A Brief History of Foraging.. 12

Why Foraging is Important.. 13

Leave No Trace.. 13

Where to Forage.. 14

Forests and Woodlands.. 14

    Meadows and Grasslands.. 15

    Coastal Areas and Beaches.. 15

    Urban Foraging.. 15

    Private Lands and Farmlands.. 16

Essential Foraging Tools.. 16

Chapter 2: Identification of Wild Edible Plants.. **19**

Plant Identification Techniques.. 20

    Morphological Plant Features.. 20

    Sensory Methods.. 20

    Habitat and Location.. 21

Seasons of Harvest.. 22

    Spring.. 22

    Summer.. 22

    Autumn.. 22

    Winter.. 22

Poisonous Plants to Avoid.. 22

    Toxic Trees and Shrubs.. 23

    Poisonous Fungi and Algae.. 23

    Symptoms of Plant Poisoning.. 25

Universal Edibility Test.. 25

Chapter 3: Edible Wild Plants.. **27**

Acer spp.. 29

Allium canadense.. 30

Allium tricoccum.. 31

Amelanchier spp.. 32

Amphicarpaea bracteata.. 33

Apios americana.. 34

Arctium iappa.. 35

Asclepias syriaca L..36

Calendula officinalis..37

Caltha palustris...38

Chenopodium album...39

Cirsium edule 40

Claytonia perfoliata 41

Crataegus monogyna..42

Elaeagnus umbellata...43

Fragaria virginiana..44

Hemerocallis fulva..45

Hydrophyllum virginianum 46

Juglans cinerea 47

Laportea canadensis 48

Matteuccia struthiopteris..49

Monarda didyma 50

Nasturtium officinale..51

Oenothera biennis...52

Opuntia spp..53

Oxalis acetosella 54

Pastinaca sativa..55

Portulaca oleracea sativa..56

Prosopis juliflora 57

Prunus pensylvanica...58

Prunus virginiana..59

Rhus spp. 60

Robinia pseudoacacia..61

Rubus spp..62

Rumex acetosella 63

Sagittaria spp..64

Sambucus canadensis..65

Smilax herbacea 66

Stellaria media 67

Taraxacum officinale...68

Tilia americana..69

Trifolium spp...70

Typha angustifolia...71

Urtica dioica..72

Vaccinium macrocarpon..73

Viburnum lentago 74

Viburnum trilobum 75

Viola sororia 76

Vitis riparia 77

Zizania aquatica, Z. palustris 78

Chapter 4: Edible Wild Mushrooms **81**

Black Trumpet (Craterellus cornucopioides) 81

Chanterelle (Cantharellus cibarius) 82

Chicken of the Woods (Laetiporus sulphureus) 83

Fairy Ring Mushroom (Marasmius oreades) 83

Giant Puffball (Calvatia gigantea) 84

Hedgehog Mushroom (Hydnum repandum) 85

Honey Mushroom (Armillaria mellea) 85

Lion's Mane (Genus Hericium) 86

Lobster Mushroom (Hypomyces lactifluorum) 86

Meadow Mushroom (Agaricus campestris) 87

Morels (Morchella spp.) 88

Oyster Mushroom (Pleurotus ostreatus) 88

Porcino (Boletus edulis) 89

Shaggy Mane (Coprinus comatus) 90

Wood Blewit (Clitocybe nuda) 90

Chapter 5: Edible Wild Seaweeds **93**

Nori (Pyropia spp.) 95

Kelp (Laminaria spp.) 96

Sea Lettuce (Ulva lactuca) 97

Dulse (Palmaria palmata) 97

Wakame (Undaria pinnatifida) 98

Irish Moss (Chondrus crispus) 99

Chapter 6: Preserving Wild Edibles **100**

Drying and Dehydrating 101

Tools and Equipment Necessary 101

Best Practices for Dehydrating Different Foods 101

Storing Dried Foods 102

Canning and Bottling 102

Water Bath vs. Pressure Canning 102

Safety Tips and Avoiding Contamination 102

Freezing Foraged Foods 103

Preparing Foods for Freezing 103

Blanching 103

Vacuum Sealing vs. Traditional Freezing Bags..103

Maximizing Freezer Storage 104

Pickling and Fermenting...104

Equipment and Ingredients..104

Pickling Process..104

Fermenting Process 105

Common Challenges and Solutions 105

Special Preparations..106

Syrups, Jams, and Jellies...106

Herbal Infusions and Teas...106

Spirits and Beverages..106

Storage Tips and Shelf Life 107

Organizing and Labelling..107

Chapter 7: Recipes **109**

Breakfast, Snacks and More (For Two) 109

Serviceberry Pancakes..109

Wild Strawberry and Raspberry Smoothie 110

Riverbank Grape Jam on Toast 110

Blueberry and Maple Syrup Compote 111

Dandelion Root Coffee..111

Wild Ginger and Blackberry Sorbet 111

Serviceberry Cobbler..112

Salads (For Two)...112

Ramps and Wild Strawberry Salad 112

Watercress and Wood Sorrel Salad...113

Dandelion and Raspberry Salad 113

Cattail and Avocado Salad...114

Main Courses (For Two)..114

Maple-Raspberry Glazed Chicken...114

Groundnut and Wild Ginger Soup 115

Sautéed Fiddleheads with Ramp...115

Purslane Stir-Fry 116

Cattail and Wild Rice Soup..116

Wild Rice and Groundnut Pilaf..117

Dandelion and Egg Frittata 117

Fiddlehead and Wild Salmon Stir-Fry...118

Dandelion and Groundnut Meatballs in Sassafras Sauce 119

Oyster Mushroom and Dandelion Fritters..119

Porcino and Ramp-Stuffed Trout 120

Morels and Watercress Pasta 120

Shaggy Mane and Purslane Stir-Fry..121

Porcino-Stuffed Chicken with Groundnut Sauce...122

Chapter 8: Foraging as A Lifestyle.. 123

Foraging as A Spiritual Practice..124

Building Community Through Foraging 125

The Future of Foraging: Challenges and Opportunities 126

Conclusion.. 129

About The Author 131

Chapter 1: Introduction to Foraging

In the embrace of nature, with the delicate whisper of leaves and the ever-present hum of life, there lies an ancient practice – foraging. Born from a synergy of necessity, spiritual communion, and innate curiosity, foraging is the age-old ritual of seeking, identifying, and collecting nature's bounty. This act, which has been instrumental for humans throughout epochs, finds renewed importance in the wake of our modern challenges: climate change, food scarcity, and an alarming loss of biodiversity.

From the heart of Georgia, where my grandparents instilled in me an enduring love for the land, to the vast expanse of our world, the traditions and techniques of foraging have been shaped and refined. This book is an amalgamation of knowledge spanning continents and cultures, weaving together indigenous insights, ancestral customs, and cutting-edge scientific research. Herein, you will journey through various terrains, learning the craft of discerning edible plants, mushrooms, and even the lesser-acknowledged nourishments nature offers. Yet, beyond the technicalities, lies a profound narrative – the cultural and spiritual tapestry that binds foraging to our very essence, and its potential to foster resilient, sustainable communities.

In our rapidly evolving world, where convenience often eclipses connection, the act of foraging beckons us to pause. To rekindle a bond with nature, to respect her offerings, and to approach with an ethic of stewardship. This isn't merely about food acquisition; it's a dance of balance, a symphony of interactions between us, the environment, and every creature that calls it home.

Utilizing the latest findings from diverse fields like ecology, biology, and environmental science, we will delve into the potential of foraging as an antidote to some of our current food system dilemmas. The emphasis is not just on sustainability, but on forging a symbiotic relationship where both humanity and nature thrive. Whether you are a novice, with tentative steps into this world, or a seasoned forager seeking deeper insights, this book aims to be your compass. It is an invitation to not just understand, but to *feel* – to imbue your foraging pursuits with mindfulness, gratitude, and a fervent commitment to a more equitable and verdant world.

Foraging is not merely an act; it's a philosophy, a way of life. A testament to our evolutionary history, and perhaps, a beacon for our future. Join me, Diane Wells, as we embark on this enriching exploration, rekindling a connection that's as old as time.

A Brief History of Foraging

Foraging, the ancient art of seeking out wild food sources, has its roots deep in our ancestral lineage. Before the dawn of agriculture, our predecessors roamed the earth, gathering edible plants as a primary means of sustenance. Seasons dictated their diets: nuts and roots were collected and stored for leaner times, while fresh fruits and vegetables were consumed immediately, relishing their fleeting abundance.

As the wheel of time turned, bringing forth the Neolithic Revolution, nomadic tribes transitioned from their wandering ways, choosing to settle and domesticate both flora and fauna. This pivotal shift transformed the sporadic act of 'foraging' into a more structured and systematic process—what we now recognize as harvesting. As early civilizations burgeoned, the notion of cultivated land solidified, evolving with the rise of the merchant societies of Antiquity. The harvest, once a communal act of gathering, morphed into an expansive industry. Tree farming and market gardening emerged, their roots tracing back to vegetable gardens of ancient times, flourishing through the Middle Ages and adapting with the sweeping changes of the Industrial Revolution.

The 19th century witnessed another metamorphosis in foraging. With the proliferation of urban allotments and private gardens, foraging transitioned from a purely rural activity to an urban one. Advances in botany coupled with an influx of specialized literature demystified plants and their myriad benefits, rekindling an interest in foraging. Urbanites, armed with newfound knowledge, often dabbled in foraging during their sojourns in the countryside, although restrictions in protected areas occasionally curtailed their endeavors.

The 20th century heralded diverse food acquisition philosophies. The 'hippie' movement of the 1960s, with its clarion call to return to nature and community-centric ideals, breathed new life into foraging. Fast forward to 2008, and the *peas & love* movement in Yorkshire epitomized communal spirit and resilience. The town of Todmorden, grappling with the clutches of recession, pioneered the Incredible Edible initiative. Residents collaboratively cultivated orchards and urban vegetable gardens, freely accessible to all. This ethos of collective consumption and support resonated globally, giving rise to around 700 similar initiatives.

Today, while many embark on foraging expeditions for sheer pleasure, there's an undeniable resurgence in its popularity. Be it the thrill of stumbling upon a delectable mushroom, the joy of identifying a forgotten herb, or the allure of unearthing a culinary gem, modern foragers are reconnecting with nature in a myriad of ways, celebrating an age-old tradition that's as much about sustenance as it is about soul.

Why Foraging is Important

From a health standpoint, foraging offers a multitude of benefits. Engaging in the act is itself an exercise; the walk, the reach, the bend, and the load carried not only enhance physical well-being but also promise mental serenity. When one immerses in nature, stress is alleviated, and a mindful connection with the environment is fostered. Moreover, the wild foods harvested—ranging from berries and nuts to roots and greens—are nutrient powerhouses, teeming with vitamins, antioxidants, and omega-3 fatty acids. Such bounty bolsters the immune system, potentially warding off illnesses, and enhancing cognitive functions.

Everyone, regardless of their background, can embrace foraging. It doesn't necessitate specialized tools or deep pockets. All it requires is a basic understanding of safety and ethical guidelines. By tapping into these naturally available resources, we not only connect with nature but also minimize food wastage and our ecological footprint.

On the cultural front, foraging serves as a bridge. It educates individuals about the ecological diversity and heritage of their surroundings. When done communally, it fosters interaction, collaboration, and exchange of ideas, weaving together the tapestry of shared experiences and traditions. Many indigenous and rural communities continue to rely on foraging, which not only sustains them nutritionally but also empowers them, granting autonomy over their resources and economy.

Leave No Trace

The "Leave No Trace" ethos is not merely an approach but a sanctified philosophy, a means to coexist harmoniously with the Earth that sustains us. The pulse of nature isn't just a metaphor but an actual rhythm, a cadence that varies from season to season, year to year. If one listens carefully, it becomes evident that nature has its own times of abundance and scarcity. For the conscientious forager, the act of harvesting is never an exploitation but rather a participation in this natural cycle. To forage ethically is to attune oneself to these rhythms, taking only what is abundant and leaving behind enough for the natural world to continue its own processes of renewal. This delicate balance is at the heart of sustainability. When we pause to consider whether our actions contribute to or detract from this balance, we elevate our practice of foraging from mere gathering to a form of ecological stewardship.

Yet, the ethos of sustainable foraging extends beyond the individual; it is deeply woven into the fabric of community. Herein lies another layer of ethical consideration: the acknowledgment and respect of the rights, traditions, and wisdom of local and indigenous communities. How tempting it is to tread where curiosity leads, yet how essential it is to pause and ponder, to secure permissions and embrace the wisdom passed down through generations. The foraging community at its best is a confluence of shared knowledge and mutual respect, where elders mentor the young, and every discovery is celebrated as a collective triumph.

Of course, this relationship with both nature and community demands vigilance for personal safety—your wellbeing watch, if you will. This is not merely about avoiding the poisonous berry or the toxic mushroom. It's about nurturing a kind of wisdom that blends caution with curiosity, equipping oneself with tools and knowledge that ensure not only successful foraging but also the long-term well-being of the ecosystems we engage with.

In a world increasingly divorced from the rhythms of nature, to forage is to remember our primal relationship with the Earth. But remembrance must be accompanied by responsibility. The ethics and sustainability of foraging are not mere checkboxes but are woven into every action we undertake in the wild. Through this lens, the "Leave No Trace" philosophy ceases to be an abstract concept; it becomes a lived reality, a way of moving through the world that honors both the fragility and the resilience of the natural systems that sustain us. And in that honoring, we don't merely take—we give back, in the form of respect, mindfulness, and a deep, abiding love for this wondrous planet that we call home.

Where to Forage

Unveiling nature's treasures requires more than just an inquisitive spirit; it demands a knowledge of where these bounties lie. As the sun casts its golden hue over meadows, forests, and coastal areas, it illuminates patches rich with edibles waiting to be discovered. The journey of foraging is as much about understanding the land as it is about the edibles themselves. Here you'll learn the best terrains, opening doors to a world of culinary and medicinal riches.

Forests and Woodlands

Tucked beneath the canopies of towering trees and set against the backdrop of rustling leaves, forests and woodlands beckon with a promise of nature's riches. This diverse ecosystem, with its layers of undergrowth and dappled sunlight, is a veritable playground for the forager. Depending on the season and the forest's geographical location, one might stumble upon patches of ripe blueberries hidden under their green foliage or the subtle scent of wild garlic wafting through the air. Autumn might unveil the treasures of hazelnuts, left forgotten by squirrels, or the elusive morel mushroom, peeking from beneath fallen leaves. The key to successful foraging in such areas lies not just in keen observation but also in understanding the forest's rhythm. Dawn, for instance, is an opportune time to forage. The morning dew, shimmering under the first rays of the sun, can highlight less-trodden paths, often leading to richer bounties. However, as with all foraging, respect for the habitat is paramount. One should tread lightly, ensuring they leave no trace behind, preserving the forest's magic for generations of foragers to come.

Meadows and Grasslands

Stretching vast and unbroken, meadows and grasslands paint a picture of nature in its most serene form. With the horizon in sight and the sky overhead, these open landscapes provide a diverse selection of edible treasures for the discerning forager. Unobstructed by dense tree canopies, sunlight bathes these terrains generously, giving life to an array of plants that thrive in open spaces. Come spring, wildflowers bloom in a riot of colors, many of which—like chamomile and dandelions—are not only beautiful to behold but offer culinary and medicinal benefits. As seasons progress, the tall grasses sway, revealing pockets of edible herbs such as wild thyme and rosemary, their fragrances carried by the wind. Nettles, often overlooked due to their sting, can be harvested and transformed into a rich soup or tea. Meadows especially, with their moist soil, can sometimes offer surprises like the wild onion or even the occasional wild strawberry patch. Just as in forests, the time of day can influence one's foraging success. Early mornings, when dew adorns the grass blades and petals, might make it easier to spot those plants that are otherwise concealed during the heat of the day.

Coastal Areas and Beaches

The sound of waves, the touch of brine on the lips, and a horizon that seems infinite — coastal areas and beaches offer more than just scenic beauty and tranquility. These marine-fringed territories are a trove of unique edible gems. Seaweeds like kelp, dulse, and sea lettuce cling to the rocks, absorbing nutrients from both sea and sunlight, waiting for the forager's hand. These marine vegetables are rich in minerals and can be an extraordinary addition to various dishes or even as standalone snacks when dried. Beyond plants, one might also find shellfish, like mussels and clams, buried just beneath the wet sands, though extreme caution and local knowledge are essential to ensure safe consumption. Coastal herbs such as sea purslane and samphire can be found sprouting amidst dunes and cliffs, adding a salty crunch to meals. However, the ocean's bounty demands respect. Always check local regulations and be aware of red tide or other contamination warnings to ensure that your seaside harvest is both bountiful and safe.

Urban Foraging

Amidst the buzz of city life, between the concrete pathways and towering skyscrapers, nature stubbornly finds its way. Urban foraging is the art of recognizing and harvesting these resilient offerings. Vacant lots, community gardens, and even your own backyard can conceal unexpected delicacies. Plants like dandelions, which many consider weeds, sprout in corners and cracks, offering both edible leaves and roots. City parks, with their wide variety of plants, can be a veritable feast for the observant forager. But urban foraging comes with its own set of challenges. It's essential to be wary of pollutants, pesticides, and other urban contaminants. Gaining permission where needed, understanding local bylaws, and practicing sustainable harvesting are paramount in these environments.

Private Lands and Farmlands

Lush private lands and expansive farmlands, with their cultivated and sometimes wild sections, can be tempting for foragers. Rows of apple trees, patches of wild berries, or the inviting sight of mushrooms after a rainy spell can be a forager's dream. But these areas come with boundaries, both seen and unseen. It's not merely about trespassing; it's about understanding and respecting the hard work farmers put into their lands. Before embarking on a foraging journey here, always seek permission. Many landowners might be open to a conversation, sometimes even providing invaluable insights about where and what to forage. They may also know areas to avoid due to pesticides or other treatments. This mutual respect and understanding can lead to a beneficial exchange for both parties. With consent, a forager can explore these lands, ensuring they harvest responsibly, always leaving enough behind, and potentially sharing their discoveries and knowledge with the landowner.

Essential Foraging Tools

As one steps into the verdant realms of nature, seeking to uncover its edible secrets, being equipped with the right tools becomes paramount. These tools not only ease the process but also ensure that foraging remains sustainable, safe, and rewarding. Each piece of equipment plays its distinctive role, marrying science, tradition, and practicality to facilitate a harmonious interaction with the wild.

The quintessential Foraging Bag or Basket serves as the trusted companion of every forager. Woven baskets, with their open structure, allow for air circulation, ensuring that the collected edibles remain fresh. The gaps between the weave also let tiny seeds, dirt, and debris fall through, naturally sifting the harvest. Bags, especially those made of breathable materials like cotton, can serve a similar purpose. Their flexibility makes them suitable for varied terrains, from dense forests to open meadows.

Next in line is the Field Guide and Identification Books. And while the book in your hands serves as a comprehensive guide, the world of foraging is vast, and regional specificity can be invaluable. These guides, often replete with images, descriptions, and habitat details, act as a bridge between the forager and the botanical world. They empower individuals with knowledge, enabling them to discern between a delightful treat and a potential threat. The illustrations and descriptions aid in confirming identifications, making them an indispensable tool, especially for beginners.

One of the most revolutionary tools available to modern foragers is the advent of mobile apps designed to identify plants through image recognition. These applications, which often leverage machine learning and vast botanical databases, allow foragers to simply snap a photo of a plant, after which the app will provide potential matches along with detailed information about each species. This near-instantaneous identification can be invaluable in the field, especially when confronted with an unfamiliar specimen.

A Knife or Scissors is more than just a cutting tool; it's an extension of the forager's intent. A sharp knife can deftly harvest plants without causing undue harm, ensuring the plant continues to thrive. Scissors, with their precise snips, are excellent for collecting delicate herbs or flowers. They allow for selective foraging, ensuring only the ripe or abundant parts are harvested, while the rest is left undisturbed, fostering sustainability.

In the vast expanses of nature, it's easy to lose oneself, both metaphorically and literally. A **GPS** becomes the anchor in such scenarios. While the allure of wandering might be enticing, having a reliable means to navigate ensures safety. Modern GPS devices, often compact and user-friendly, can help foragers mark specific spots, be it a bountiful patch of berries or a rare medicinal herb. For those inclined towards tradition, a compass, coupled with basic navigational skills, can be equally effective.

Finally, the humble Notebook and Pen might seem archaic in a digital age, but its value is timeless. Documenting personal experiences, sketching an unknown plant, jotting down the location of a particular patch, or simply penning down reflections – the notebook becomes the canvas. It evolves into a personalized field guide, capturing the nuances of each foraging expedition. Over time, it transforms into a chronicle, bearing witness to the forager's journey, growth, and the ever-evolving relationship with nature.

Armed with these tools, a forager is not just equipped but empowered. They stand at the confluence of the ancient and the modern, ready to delve into nature's pantry with respect, curiosity, and a sense of wonder.

☆ ☆ ☆ ☆ ☆

SUBMIT A REVIEW

If you enjoyed this chapter, I would be grateful if you could support me by leaving a review of the book on Amazon. Your feedback is very valuable and inspires me!

It's very simple and only takes a few minutes:

1. Go to the "My Orders" page on Amazon and search for the book "Forager's Harvest 101".

2. Select "Write a product review".

3. Select a Star Rating.

4. Optionally, add text, photos, or videos and select Submit.

Chapter 2: Identification of Wild Edible Plants

Identifying plants accurately stands at the crux of successful foraging. The very act of foraging taps into our most primal instincts, tracing back to times when our ancestors roamed the earth, gathering wild foods. Yet, the landscape has shifted, and in today's world where supermarkets simplify choices, many have lost the innate knowledge once held about the natural world. Venturing into the wilderness without the proper ability to discern one plant from another can have severe, sometimes fatal, consequences. Edible and toxic plants can be deceptively similar, making it perilously easy to mistake one for the other. For instance, the innocuous-looking Wild Carrot (Daucus carota) shares an uncanny resemblance with the deadly Poison Hemlock (Conium maculatum).

A simple misstep in identification can lead to ingesting harmful toxins instead of nourishing sustenance. The importance of plant identification extends beyond just individual safety. As foragers, there's a responsibility to protect and preserve the very environment that offers its bounty. Accurate identification ensures that only the intended plants are harvested, preserving the delicate balance of ecosystems. Misidentification can lead to the unintended collection of rare or endangered species, further pushing them towards the brink of extinction. Conservation isn't just about leaving no trace; it's about ensuring that the footprints left behind are of informed and conscientious steps. An informed forager not only safeguards their well-being but contributes to the broader health of the planet, ensuring that wild spaces continue to flourish and provide for generations to come.

Plant Identification Techniques

Morphological Plant Features

Diving into plant identification, one quickly realizes that nature provides a myriad of clues, subtly hinting at the identity of each plant. Among the most reliable of these clues are the morphological features of plants, tangible aspects that we can see, touch, and sometimes even taste or smell.

Leaves, often the most accessible parts of plants, are rife with details. Their shapes can range from the simple ovals of some oaks to the intricate lobes of maples. Margins, or the edges of leaves, too offer clues. Some might be smooth, called entire, while others can be toothed, serrated, or even lobed. Observing how leaves attach to stems, known as their arrangement, can be equally revealing. They might be opposite, alternating, or even whorled in their layout. The intricate network of veins on a leaf, its venation, can also be a crucial identifier, with patterns ranging from pinnate to palmate. Lastly, the color of leaves, especially in seasons other than spring, can vary widely and provides hints, especially when looking at undersides which might differ in hue.

Stems, while often overlooked, can be treasure troves of information. Some might be smooth, while others might be covered in tiny hairs, known as trichomes. In certain plants, the stems may bear thorns or spines, immediately narrowing down potential species. The general structure, whether herbaceous and soft or woody and hard, gives away much about a plant's identity and its life cycle.

Flowers, with their vibrant allure, are among nature's most conspicuous signs. Their colors can be a direct giveaway, but it's often the more subtle characteristics that are crucial. The size of the flower, the specific shape of its petals, and its arrangement, whether solitary or clustered, can all provide significant insights. For example, the umbrella-like clusters of the carrot family or the composite heads of the daisy family are unique and distinctive.

Then come the fruits and seeds, which not only carry life but also tales of the plants they come from. Their colors can be indicative, but it's often characteristics like size, texture, and even taste that offer the most accurate insights. A word of caution here: tasting is a method left to those deeply familiar with plants, as certain species can be toxic. The very structure, whether a berry, drupe, or legume, can instantly guide an identifier in the right direction.

Lastly, the roots, often hidden from plain sight, bear unique characteristics. Their very structure, whether fibrous, taproot, or rhizomatous, can be revealing. The color of roots can vary from the pale whites and yellows to deep browns and even blacks. Certain roots, especially among herbs, exude distinctive smells when crushed or broken, immediately hinting at their identity.

Sensory Methods

Beyond the visual cues that plants offer, nature beckons foragers to lean in closer and engage other senses to unlock the mysteries of plant identities. By weaving together the impressions captured through smell, touch, and taste, a more profound understanding of the botanical world emerges. Some plants emit fragrances so distinctive that even with closed eyes, one can name them. The fresh, piercing scent of mint or the earthy aroma of sage are just a couple of instances. Smell serves dual purposes. Recognizing these distinctive smells can act as a swift identifier, narrowing down a plant's identity, especially when combined with other clues.

Touch brings us closer to plants, allowing us to feel their world. The soft fuzz on a sage leaf, the sticky residue of a pine needle, or the cool, smooth surface of a succulent all guide our understanding. Yet, this method calls for prudence, because some plants could be irritants. Touching plants like poison ivy or stinging nettle can lead to immediate and uncomfortable reactions. As such, familiarity and caution go hand in hand, ensuring that the forager's curiosity does not lead to undesirable consequences.

Taste should be approached with the utmost respect and caution. Plants, like all living beings, have evolved defense mechanisms, and some have developed toxins that can be harmful or even fatal if consumed. Before ever considering tasting a wild plant, it must be conclusively identified using other means. Only then, and if certain of its edibility, should one venture a taste. Even then, it's advised to try only a tiny bit initially to check for any adverse reactions (please refer to the Universal Edibility Test). The nuanced flavors of wild plants can range from the sharp bite of wild garlic to the sweet tang of wild berries, each offering a direct connection to the land it sprouted from.

Habitat and Location

Forests, with their dappled sunlight filtering through the canopy, provide shelter to a myriad of shade-loving plants. Here, one might find plants that have evolved broad leaves to capture as much sunlight as possible. These leaves may have a waxy coat, serving as protection against the dampness that a closed canopy might trap. In contrast, meadows are open spaces, often bathed in sunlight, and house plants that thrive in direct sunlight, exhibiting vibrant flowers designed to attract pollinators in such a competitive environment. Wetlands, areas perpetually or seasonally saturated with water, become home to plants that have developed adaptations to survive in waterlogged conditions.

These plants might display aerenchyma, specialized tissues that allow them to transfer oxygen from the atmosphere to their submerged roots. Deserts, on the opposite spectrum, with their arid conditions, host plants that have mastered water conservation. Succulents, with their fleshy leaves that store water, or plants with deep taproots to access groundwater, become iconic of such habitats. But it isn't just the broad habitat types that influence plant distribution. The very soil they anchor themselves in can be a determinant of their presence. Some plants prefer acidic soils, often found under coniferous forests, while others may thrive in alkaline conditions, like those seen in coastal regions with limestone rocks. The texture of the soil, be it sandy, loamy, or clayey, can also dictate which plants flourish. Certain plants have evolved to extract nutrients from poor soils, while others are found in rich, fertile grounds, often near riverbanks or floodplains.

Altitude too weaves its influence into this tapestry. As one ascends a mountain, the drop in temperature and atmospheric pressure brings about a change in the plant community. Lower altitudes might see lush forests, but as one climbs higher, these give way to hardier shrubs and, eventually, to alpine meadows with dwarf plants that have evolved to withstand the harsh conditions of high elevations.

Seasons of Harvest

Here are some examples of edible plants that can be foraged across different seasons.

Spring

Allium canadense, Allium tricoccum, Amelanchier spp., Calendula officinalis, Caltha palustris, Claytonia perforate, Crataegus monogyna, Fragaria virginiana, Hydrophyllum virginianum, Matteuccia struthiopteris, Nasturtium officinale, Oxalis acetosella, Stellaria media, Taraxacum officinale, Viola sororia.

Summer

Acer spp., Amphicarpaea bracteate, Apios americana, Asclepias syriaca L., Chenopodium album, Cirsium edule, Elaeagnus umbellate, Hemerocallis fulva, Juglans cinerea, Laportea canadensis, Monarda didyma, Oenothera biennis, Opuntia spp., Pastinaca sativa, Portulaca oleracea sativa, Prunus pensylvanica, Rhus spp., Rumex acetosella, Sagittaria spp., Sambucus canadensis, Smilax herbacea, Trifolium spp., Urtica dioica, Vaccinium macrocarpon.

Autumn

Amelanchier spp. (late varieties or for berries), Arctium iappa Juglans cinerea (nuts), Prosopis juliflora (seeds/pods), Prunus virginiana (for fruits), Robinia pseudoacacia (seeds), Rubus spp. (some varieties might still be bearing fruit), Typha angustifolia (seeds), Viburnum lentago (berries), Viburnum trilobum (berries), Vitis riparia, Zizania aquatica, Z. palustris (wild rice).

Winter

Acer spp. (for tapping maple syrup, depending on the specific type and region), Arctium iappa (roots), Pastinaca sativa (roots), Tilia americana (for bark or twigs in late winter).

Poisonous Plants to Avoid

As we delve into understanding plant toxicity, it's crucial to differentiate between toxicity, irritants, and allergens. Toxicity refers to the inherent ability of a substance to cause harm, often through ingestion, leading to poisoning. On the other hand, irritants are compounds that may cause inflammation or discomfort, usually on contact, without necessarily being toxic when ingested. For example, touching the sap of certain plants can result in skin rashes, even if consuming that same plant might be harmless. Allergens are a unique category, representing substances that might be harmless to most but can trigger an immune response in susceptible individuals, often resulting in allergic reactions that can range from mild rashes to severe anaphylaxis. Now, one might wonder, why would plants develop these compounds in the first place? The answer lies in evolution and the constant battle for survival. Many plants have evolved toxic compounds as a defense mechanism against herbivores, deterring animals from consuming them. These protective measures, developed over millennia, ensure that the plant species can continue to thrive and reproduce without constant threat from hungry predators.

From mildly noxious flora to deadly poisonous specimens, the range is vast and frequently surprising. Some plants, although toxic in certain parts, can also have nourishing edible sections. An intriguing detail lies in how the toxic effects of certain plants are neutralized through specific preparation methods, such as boiling or fermenting. The age of the plant can play a significant role as well. A plant that might be dangerous at one stage of its life cycle can be entirely safe at another. Furthermore, many toxic plants possess a beguiling beauty or closely resemble their benign counterparts, potentially misleading an uninformed forager into making a risky choice.

Toxic Trees and Shrubs

One of the most notable among toxic trees is the yew tree. While this evergreen might look unassuming, almost every part of it, especially the seeds, is deadly if ingested, containing a compound called taxine that can lead to cardiac arrest. Ironically, the only safe part of this tree is its red, fleshy aril which surrounds the seed, a tempting treat for birds who discard the toxic seed within. The locust tree provides a lesson in deceptive appearances. Its fragrant white flowers are edible when cooked (as discussed in this book). However, other parts of the locust tree, especially the bark and shoots, contain a toxin called robin's robin, which can cause nausea, weakness, and even death in severe cases.

Venturing lower, to the shrubs, we encounter the likes of the oleander. Often used for ornamental purposes because of its stunning white, pink, or red flowers, every part of the oleander is lethal. Its leaves and stems contain several toxic compounds like oleandrin and neriine that can affect the heart and the digestive system, leading to symptoms ranging from vomiting and diarrhea to irregular heartbeats.

Similarly deceptive is the elderberry shrub. While the flowers, ripe black or blue berries of some elderberry species are often used in pies and jams, their leaves, stems, and even the seeds within the berries contain cyanogenic glycosides. These compounds can release cyanide when digested, leading to a variety of symptoms like nausea, vomiting, and more severe metabolic and respiratory distress if consumed in large quantities.

Another shrub to be wary of is the daphne. Its berries might look tantalizing, especially to children, with their bright colors and fleshy appearance. But consuming even a few can lead to serious complications due to the toxic compounds they contain, resulting in symptoms ranging from a burning sensation in the mouth and throat to a drastic drop in blood pressure.

Poisonous Fungi and Algae

Mushrooms, the fruiting bodies of certain fungi, have long been sought after for their culinary attributes and medicinal properties. Yet, hidden among the delectable chanterelles and prized truffles are those like the death cap and the destroying angel. These sinister-sounding fungi, Amanita phalloides and Amanita virosa respectively, are well-named. Consuming even a small portion can lead to severe liver and kidney damage and can be fatal if not treated promptly. Their toxins, notably amatoxins, are not destroyed by cooking, and their effects can be delayed, giving the victim a false sense of safety before symptoms like vomiting, diarrhea, and abdominal pain set in.

Death Cap (Amanita phalloides)

Destroying Angel (Amanita bisporigera)

The world beneath the waves is no less treacherous when it comes to toxic organisms. Marine algae, though responsible for producing a significant portion of the world's oxygen and serving as a primary food source in marine ecosystems, can sometimes bloom uncontrollably, leading to events known as harmful algal blooms (HABs). During these episodes, certain species of algae release potent toxins that can poison marine life and, indirectly, humans who consume affected seafood. For instance, dinoflagellates, tiny photosynthetic organisms, can produce toxins that lead to conditions like paralytic shellfish poisoning (PSP), neurotoxic shellfish poisoning (NSP), and ciguatera fish poisoning (CFP). Notably, these organisms can cause "red tides" or harmful algal blooms, with coastal waters appearing reddish-brown as an indicator of their presence.

The resulting conditions can manifest as a range of symptoms from numbness and tingling to digestive disturbances, and in severe cases, respiratory paralysis. Moreover, the threat of toxic algae isn't limited to marine environments. Freshwater blooms, often dominated by cyanobacteria (sometimes referred to as blue-green algae), can produce a variety of toxins affecting the liver and nervous system. These cyanobacteria can often be identified in freshwater by their greenish-blue, sometimes slimy appearance, forming thick mats on the water's surface. Swimmers and recreational users of affected waters, or even pets drinking from these sources, can experience skin irritations, allergic reactions, and if ingested, more severe health implications.

Symptoms of Plant Poisoning

Ingesting toxic plants can elicit a range of symptoms, often beginning mildly but potentially escalating in severity. These manifestations vary based on the particular toxin involved, the quantity consumed, and individual sensitivities. Initial reactions might include a tingling or burning sensation on the lips, tongue, or throat. In some cases, this can progress to more intense oral irritation, excessive salivation, and difficulty swallowing.

Stomach upset, often presenting as nausea or vomiting, is another common symptom. It may be accompanied by diarrhea, cramping, and abdominal pain. Certain plant toxins can lead to a drastic drop in blood pressure, manifesting as dizziness, blurred vision, or even fainting. On the neurological front, symptoms might encompass headaches, disorientation, tremors, seizures, or in extreme cases, unconsciousness.

Some toxic plants interfere with heart function, leading to palpitations, arrhythmias, or even cardiac arrest. Others might have a diuretic effect, causing excessive thirst and urination. There's also the possibility of experiencing difficulty in breathing, either due to throat swelling or direct impacts on respiratory function.In the event of skin contact with certain toxic plants, symptoms can be externally evident too. This might range from mild irritation, itching, or rashes to severe blisters or chemical burns.

When plant poisoning is suspected, swift action is essential. First, remove any remnants of the plant from the mouth and immediately contact emergency services, especially if the individual is unconscious, experiencing difficulty breathing, or displaying severe symptoms. For those conscious and coherent, it helps to identify the plant responsible, either by gathering a sample or taking a clear photograph. This aids healthcare professionals in determining the best course of action. Activated charcoal can be a useful first-aid measure since it binds to many toxins, preventing further absorption into the bloodstream. However, it's crucial to consult with a healthcare professional or poison control center before administering any treatment or remedy.

In all cases of suspected plant poisoning, it's imperative to seek medical attention promptly. Even if symptoms seem mild or are receding, some toxins have delayed effects or can cause long-term damage if not appropriately addressed. Remember, the natural world is abundant with wonders, but it demands our respect and caution. Knowledge, preparation, and prompt action are our best allies in navigating its challenges.

Universal Edibility Test

The Universal Edibility Test emerges as a beacon for foragers, a systematic procedure designed to identify which plants are safe to eat and which are not. While the test is invaluable, it is crucial to approach it with patience, as it is both time-consuming and demands meticulous observation.

The premise of the test lies in the understanding that our bodies often give subtle signals when confronted with potential toxins. By isolating plant parts and introducing them gradually, foragers can monitor their body's reactions, discerning edibility through methodical progression. The test begins with segregating the plant into its primary components: leaves, stems, roots, buds, and flowers. It's vital to remember that just because one part of a plant is edible, it doesn't guarantee the edibility of the whole. For example, while the leaves of a plant might be nutritious and delicious, its berries could be toxic. With the plant divided, the forager then selects a single component to test.

The chosen part is first held against the inner side of the wrist or elbow for a few minutes to check for any immediate allergic reactions, like itching or redness. If the skin remains unchanged, the next step is to prepare the plant part as they would for consumption, typically by boiling. Once prepared, the forager places a small piece of the plant component against their lips, waiting for about 15 minutes. If there's no burning or itching sensation, they then move the piece to the tongue, holding it there for another 15 minutes, ensuring they do not swallow. If this too doesn't yield any adverse reactions, they chew it slowly, again without swallowing, observing for any numbing or unsettling sensations. If all seems well up to this point, the forager swallows the tiny morsel and waits. This waiting is essential, and it can range from a few hours to an entire day. The body needs time to process and react to potential toxins. If after this duration, the forager feels perfectly normal with no nausea, dizziness, stomach cramps, or any other discomfort, they can tentatively classify that specific plant part as edible. It's essential to repeat this procedure for each component of the plant, always ensuring there's no mixing, to isolate any reactions and pinpoint edibility accurately. Also, it's worth noting that the Universal Edibility Test is a guideline for unknown plants. Whenever possible, foragers should prioritize learning from local experts and relying on trusted field guides, as these resources offer time-tested wisdom, often saving time and potentially preventing harm.

To understand the real-world application of this test, consider the wild potato. Its tubers, when prepared correctly, can be a delightful source of nutrition. However, its berries and leaves can be harmful if consumed. Another example is the elderberry tree. While its flowers and ripe berries, especially when cooked, are famed for syrups and pies, its leaves, stems, and unripe berries contain toxic compounds. The Universal Edibility Test would help differentiate between these contrasting edibilities, ensuring safe and informed foraging.

★ ★ ★ ★ ★

SUBMIT A REVIEW

If you enjoyed this chapter, I would be grateful if you could support me by leaving a review of the book on Amazon. Your feedback is very valuable and inspires me!

It's very simple and only takes a few minutes:

1. Go to the "My Orders" page on Amazon and search for the book "Forager's Harvest 101".
2. Select "Write a product review".
3. Select a Star Rating.
4. Optionally, add text, photos, or videos and select Submit.

Chapter 3: Edible Wild Plants

While every endeavor has been undertaken to present accurate and reliable information within this book, I must emphasize that I cannot assume responsibility for any adverse effects that may emerge from the employment of the plants detailed, be it for culinary, medicinal, or other uses. The knowledge shared in these pages stems from a tapestry of experiences—both those cherished moments with my grandparents and the insights gathered over years of intimate interactions with the natural world—as well as meticulous studies, rigorous research, and, in this digital age, invaluable web sources. It's my ardent hope that this compilation serves to deepen your appreciation and understanding of the enchanting domain of botany. However, I beseech you, dear reader, to not interpret this information as unequivocal endorsements for consumption or application. The intricate tapestry of the botanical world is as layered and multifaceted as it is alluring, with certain species concealing components that could be detrimental. Thus, before venturing to utilize any plant, whether for nourishment, healing, or other endeavors, it's of the utmost importance to engage in thorough research, possibly seeking counsel from seasoned professionals, especially if you find yourself navigating specific health scenarios such as diabetes, pregnancy, or the care of young ones. Your well-being, and that of those you hold dear, stands paramount. And while the alchemy of cooking can often mitigate certain undesirable elements in many species, prudence remains a cherished companion. As you journey through the botanical tapestry, may you do so with a heart brimming with curiosity, yet tempered by caution.

MOBILE PHOTO-GALLERY

SCAN THE QR CODE

SCAN THE QR CODE

Or click the link: https://bit.ly/3FOgxBl

Acer spp.

Common Name: Maple Trees

Family: Sapindaceae

Description: Acer, commonly referred to as Maple trees, are a diverse genus within the Sapindaceae family. These deciduous or evergreen trees are best known for their stunning autumn foliage, which runs the gamut from vibrant yellows to fiery reds. Maple trees can grow from 10 to 45 meters, depending on the species. Most maples bear small flowers in various arrangements and shades—typically yellow, green, or red—which develop into the characteristic winged fruits known as samaras. These trees are generally hermaphroditic, featuring both male and female reproductive parts, making them predominantly wind-pollinated. They are an iconic symbol of the fall season and often serve as focal points in landscapes and natural habitats.

Known Hazards: Some species may produce sap that's an irritant to certain individuals. While the sap is generally safe and is even used to make maple syrup, always ensure you're dealing with a non-toxic species before consumption.

Habitats: Maples are highly adaptable trees that flourish in a variety of soils and climates. From urban yards to deep forests, uplands to lowlands, their versatility is remarkable. Some species prefer moist, well-drained soil, while others are more drought-tolerant.

Range: The natural range of the Acer genus is primarily in the Northern Hemisphere, spanning North America, Europe, North Africa, and Asia. Some species have been introduced to other parts of the world, including Australia.

Identification: Identifying a maple tree involves recognizing its characteristic features. Most have palmately lobed leaves, with the number of lobes varying by species. The leaves are well-known for their vivid autumn colors, transitioning from greens to a palette of yellows, oranges, and reds. Small flowers appear in early spring, usually before or simultaneous with the unfolding of the leaves. The winged samaras are also distinctive to maples; these fruits whirl through the air when falling, aiding in their dispersion. The bark is generally smooth in younger trees, becoming furrowed and textured with age. Crush a leaf or samara, and you may detect a subtle but distinctive scent, varying by species.

Edible Uses: The culinary uses of maple trees are centered around their sap, which is tapped primarily in the spring. When reduced, it yields maple syrup, a staple in many kitchens. Young leaves of some species are edible and can be added to salads or cooked as greens. The seeds inside the samaras are edible when young but tend to become bitter as they mature.

Medicinal Uses: The medicinal benefits of the Acer genus are mostly derived from the sap. It has been traditionally used as a spring tonic, aimed to revitalize and invigorate after a long winter. The inner bark, when dried and made into a tea, is known to have astringent and sedative properties. It has been used in traditional medicine for treating coughs, diarrhea, and other minor ailments. Some species have leaves that, when made into a poultice, can treat skin irritations and minor wounds. Always consult a healthcare provider before beginning any new medicinal regimen.

Allium canadense

Common Name: Wild Garlic, Meadow Garlic, Canadian Garlic

Family: Amaryllidaceae

Description: Allium canadense, commonly known as Wild Garlic or Meadow Garlic, is a perennial herbaceous plant belonging to the Amaryllidaceae family. This North American native typically stands about 30-60 cm tall and displays white, pink, or lavender flowers in late spring to early summer. The plant's bulbs and bulbils are the primary modes of reproduction, although it is also capable of seed production. While it often grows in clumps and can spread aggressively, it offers a unique blend of ecological benefits and culinary opportunities.

Known Hazards: Overconsumption can lead to digestive issues and may lead to stronger body odor due to its high sulfur content. Ensure you are correctly identifying the plant, as it can resemble other toxic species.

Habitats: Preferring well-drained soils, Wild Garlic thrives in a variety of environments, from meadows and open woodlands to grasslands and even disturbed soils. It tends to favor areas with adequate sunlight but can tolerate partial shade.

Range: This species is native to a wide swath of North America, including most of the United States and parts of Canada. It is especially prevalent in the Eastern and Central U.S.

Identification: Identifying Allium canadense involves recognizing its narrow, grass-like leaves and bulbous root structure. The leaves are linear, tapering, and hollow, providing a very garlic-like aroma when crushed. Its flower head is an umbel, containing multiple small six-petaled flowers, which can vary in color. Beneath the soil, you'll find a bulb that's reminiscent of garlic or onions, encased in a membranous outer layer. Crush any part of the plant, and you'll be met with an unmistakable garlic scent, a defining characteristic of Allium canadense.

Edible Uses: The entire plant is edible, offering an array of culinary uses. The bulbs can be used just like garlic or shallots, providing a robust flavor to dishes. The tender leaves are also edible and can be chopped into salads, used as a garnish, or cooked like greens. The flowers, too, are a flavorful and decorative addition to culinary creations.

Medicinal Uses: Like other members of the Allium genus, Wild Garlic has a range of potential health benefits. Its bulbs are rich in sulfur compounds, known for their antiseptic and antibiotic properties. Consuming the plant may aid in reducing blood pressure and cholesterol levels, although medical consultation is advised. A poultice of the crushed bulbs can be applied to insect bites or minor wounds to mitigate infection. However, it's crucial to consult with healthcare professionals before starting any new medicinal regimen.

Other Uses: The ornamental appeal of this wild onion's flower clusters makes it a favorite in butterfly gardens. The plant is also known to be a natural insect repellent, driving away common pests like aphids and moles.

Allium tricoccum

Common Name: Ramps, Wild Leek, Wood Leek

Family: Amaryllidaceae

Description: Allium tricoccum, commonly known as ramps or wild leeks, are perennial woodland plants, notable for their broad, lance-shaped leaves and strong garlic-onion scent. They emerge early in spring and are one of the first signs of the awakening forest floor. Ramps have become increasingly popular in culinary circles due to their unique flavor, which blends the tastes of garlic and onion.

Known Hazards: Consumed in moderate amounts, ramps are generally safe. However, like many plants in the Allium genus, they should be eaten in moderation, as excessive consumption might lead to digestive discomfort.

Habitats: Ramps favor moist, deciduous forests and thrive in rich, well-draining soil. They are often found in patches and are particularly abundant near the eastern coast of North America, especially in the Appalachian region.

Range: Allium tricoccum is native to the eastern North American mountains, from Georgia to Canada.

Identification: Identifying ramps is relatively easy due to their distinct broad, lance-shaped leaves that appear in early spring. When crushed or chopped, the leaves emit a strong garlic-onion aroma, a defining characteristic of the plant. Later in the season, after the leaves have withered, a single flower stalk emerges from each bulb, capped with an umbel of white flowers. The underground bulb is white, often with purple or burgundy tints on the lower stem.

Edible Uses: Both the leaves and the bulbs of the ramps can be eaten. They can be consumed raw, where they have a spicy, pungent flavor, or cooked, where they impart a mild, sweet onion-garlic flavor to dishes. Ramps are a prized ingredient in gourmet cooking and are often used in salads, soups, and stir-fries. The bulbs can also be pickled.

Medicinal Uses: Indigenous peoples of North America have historically used ramps for various medicinal purposes. They were believed to purify the blood and used as an expectorant. The juice of the plant was also used as an insect repellent, and a poultice made from the leaves was applied to insect bites and stings.

Amelanchier spp.

Common Name: Serviceberry, Shadbush, Juneberry, Saskatoon

Family: Rosaceae

Description: Amelanchier, commonly known as Serviceberry or Juneberry, is a genus containing several species of deciduous shrubs and small trees. These plants are renowned for their showy white blossoms during the spring, often before many other trees have leafed out. The flowers give way to small, round, and usually sweet berries, which shift from red to a dark purplish-black when ripe. They are often a treat for both humans and wildlife alike. The genus is celebrated for its versatile uses, appealing both in ornamental and culinary contexts.

Known Hazards: The seeds of some species might contain cyanogenic glycosides which can release cyanide when ingested. Though the quantity is generally small and not harmful when consumed in moderation, excessive ingestion, especially of the seeds, should be avoided.

Habitats: Serviceberries are predominantly found in woodlands, by streams or wetlands, and on rocky hillsides. They favor well-draining soil and can thrive both in full sun or partial shade.

Range: This genus has a wide distribution across North America, with species variations being found from the northernmost parts of Canada to the southern areas of the U.S.

Identification: Amelanchier plants are best identified by their characteristic five-petaled white flowers that appear in early spring. These flowers cluster in racemes, creating a delightful show. As the seasons progress, watch out for the edible berries which mature around June. The leaves of most species are elliptical and serrated, turning a fiery red or orange in the fall. The bark of mature trees is smooth and gray, sometimes exhibiting a slightly striped or checkered pattern.

Edible Uses: The berries are the highlight when it comes to edibility. They can be consumed raw, baked into pies, made into jams, or even turned into wine. Their sweet and slightly almond-like flavor is a summer treat. In some species, the roasted seed can be a substitute for coffee.

Medicinal Uses: Historically, various indigenous tribes have used parts of the serviceberry plant for medicinal purposes, often as a digestive aid or to treat ailments like a sore throat. However, its primary use in modern times is culinary rather than medicinal.

Amphicarpaea bracteata

Common Name: Hog Peanut, American Hog Peanut

Family: Fabaceae

Description: Amphicarpaea bracteata, or Hog Peanut, is a twining annual herb belonging to the Fabaceae family. This vining plant displays delicate, trifoliate leaves and bears both aerial and subterranean flowers. The aerial flowers are small and pinkish to lavender, typically blooming in late summer, giving way to flat seed pods. The subterranean flowers don't open but self-pollinate, producing a peanut-like, edible tuber. It can grow to a length of up to 6 feet, depending on support and conditions.

Known Hazards: There are no significant known hazards related to this plant; however, those with peanut allergies may want to exercise caution.

Habitats: This plant enjoys moist, well-drained soils and thrives in both full sun and partial shade. You will often find it along streams, woodlands, and in thickets.

Range: Native to Eastern and Central North America, its range extends from Quebec down to Georgia and as far west as the Great Plains.

Identification: Hog Peanut can be identified by its trifoliate leaves, resembling those of a clover but larger. During late summer, look for its delicate, pink to lavender aerial flowers that are arranged in loose racemes. The unique feature is its production of both aerial and subterranean flowers, with the latter producing the "hog peanuts" or edible tubers.

Edible Uses: The aerial seed pods can be consumed and have a flavor akin to soybeans. They can be boiled or eaten raw. The underground tubers, resembling peanuts, are also edible and can be eaten raw or cooked. They are nutty in flavor and can be harvested in the fall.

Medicinal Uses: While there is not much documented medicinal use for Amphicarpaea bracteata, some Native American tribes have historically used it as a food source and to treat minor digestive complaints. As always, consult healthcare professionals before considering any plant for medicinal uses.

Apios americana

Common Name: Groundnut, Indian Potato, Hopniss

Family: Fabaceae

Description: Apios americana, popularly known as the Groundnut or Indian Potato, is a perennial climbing vine native to North America. It belongs to the Fabaceae family and grows up to 3 meters long, often twining around other plants or structures. Its pinnate leaves comprise 5-7 leaflets and are rich green in color. During late summer, it blossoms with fragrant, bicolored flowers that range from maroon to pinkish-brown. The plant produces edible tubers, which can be harvested in late fall or winter. Apios americana is a nitrogen-fixing plant, beneficial to the soil and surrounding flora.

Known Hazards: Although generally safe when cooked, the tubers may cause flatulence or digestive upset in some individuals. Consuming the plant raw is not recommended.

Habitats: The Groundnut favors moist, well-drained soil conditions and is often found near water bodies such as streams, rivers, and lakes. It prefers full to partial sun and is tolerant of some shade.

Range: Native to Eastern and Central North America, its range extends from Southern Canada down to Florida and as far west as the Rocky Mountains.

Identification: To identify Apios americana, look for its distinct pinnate leaves, climbing habit, and clusters of fragrant flowers. The tubers are roughly the size and shape of a finger joint, found connected in strings beneath the soil surface. They have a somewhat rough, brown skin and a firm, creamy interior. The flowers, which are shaped like typical legume family blooms, are an easily recognizable feature, usually appearing in dense racemes.

Edible Uses: The tubers of Apios americana are its most commonly consumed part, providing a starchy, nutty flavor. They can be boiled, roasted, or even dried and ground into flour. Young seedpods and seeds can also be cooked and eaten, though they are less commonly utilized. The cooked tubers are a good source of protein and various nutrients, such as iron and phosphorus.

Medicinal Uses: Although not as well-documented for medicinal use as some other native plants, Groundnut has traditionally been used by Native Americans for a variety of ailments. The tubers are said to have diuretic properties and have been employed in treatments for urinary and kidney issues. A poultice made from the boiled tubers can be applied to bruises and rheumatic areas for relief. As always, it is advisable to consult healthcare professionals before using any plant for medicinal purposes.

Other Uses: The fibrous stems of groundnut were traditionally used by Native Americans for making textiles and ropes.

Arctium iappa

Common Name: Burdock, Greater Burdock, Gobo

Family: Asteraceae

Description: Burdock, prominently recognized as Gobo in Japanese cuisine, is a biennial plant hailing from the Asteraceae family. It prominently stands with large, broad leaves and can reach heights of 1 to 2 meters. By its second year, the plant showcases purple thistle-like flowers that mature into burrs, which are notably prickly and can easily cling to fur or clothing.

Known Hazards: While the root is widely consumed, it's important to note that Burdock's leaves and flower stalks contain low levels of compounds that can be harmful if consumed in large quantities. Always ensure the proper part is being consumed and avoid excessive intake. Importantly, Burdock seeds contain polyacetylenes, which can be toxic when ingested in large amounts, leading to symptoms like dry mouth, dilated pupils, and even hallucinations.

Habitats: Burdock thrives in various habitats, notably along roadsides, vacant lots, and woodland edges. It has a preference for disturbed grounds and is often considered a weed in many gardens and cultivated lands.

Range: Originally native to Europe and Asia, Burdock has since naturalized in parts of North America.

Identification: The hallmark of Burdock is its bristly seed heads or burrs. These burrs are often a method of dispersal, as they hitch rides on animals or human clothing. In its flowering stage during the second year, Burdock sports purplish flowers that appear in clusters atop its tall stems. The plant's deep roots are brownish-green, or nearly black on the outside.

Edible Uses: Burdock root, or Gobo, is a staple in Asian cuisine. It can be peeled, sliced, and then eaten raw or cooked. The taste is crisp and mildly sweet, often likened to that of artichokes. Young stems and leaves can also be consumed after boiling to remove bitterness. In Japan, the roots are stir-fried, pickled, or added to soups.

Medicinal Uses: Traditionally, Burdock root has been regarded as a diuretic and blood-purifying agent. It's also been used for skin conditions like eczema, acne, and psoriasis. The seeds are used in traditional Chinese medicine for their alleged detoxifying effects. Always consult with a healthcare professional before using plants for medicinal purposes.

Asclepias syriaca L.

Common Name: Common Milkweed

Family: Apocynaceae

Description: Asclepias syriaca, known as Common Milkweed, is a perennial plant recognized by its broad leaves and intricate, ball-shaped pinkish-purple flowers. Reaching heights of up to 2 meters, this plant plays a crucial role in the lifecycle of the Monarch butterfly, serving both as a primary food source for caterpillars and a nectar source for adults.

Known Hazards: The milky latex of Common Milkweed contains cardiac glycosides, which can be toxic when ingested in large amounts. This plant should be consumed with caution and preferably only after thorough cooking. Additionally, the sap can be a skin irritant for some individuals.

Habitats: Favoring full sunlight, Asclepias syriaca typically thrives in sandy or loamy soils and prefers well-drained conditions. It's often found in open fields, meadows, and along roadsides.

Range: This plant is native to eastern and central North America, spanning from Quebec and New England to the Dakotas, and south to Kansas and Virginia.

Identification: To identify Asclepias syriaca, look for its characteristic milky sap when any part of the plant is broken or damaged. The combination of its broad leaves and unique clusters of pinkish-purple flowers is also distinctive.

Edible Uses: Young shoots, leaves, flower buds, and immature fruits of the Common Milkweed are edible when cooked. They can be boiled and consumed like greens. The silky floss from mature seed pods has also been used historically as a sugar substitute after being processed.

Medicinal Uses: Historically, Native American tribes utilized Common Milkweed for various medicinal purposes, including as an expectorant, a remedy for respiratory issues, and as a treatment for warts. The plant's milky latex was also applied to warts and corns. However, its use in modern herbal medicine is limited, and caution is advised due to its potential toxicity.

Other Uses: The silky hairs attached to the seeds, often referred to as "floss", have been used as a stuffing material and can serve as a fire starter. The strong fibers in the plant's stem can be extracted and used to create twine or rope. Additionally, Common Milkweed is essential for butterfly gardening, particularly for those looking to support Monarch butterflies.

Calendula officinalis

Common Name: Pot Marigold, Common Marigold, English Marigold

Family: Asteraceae

Description: Calendula officinalis, commonly known as Pot Marigold, is an annual or short-lived perennial herb that is a distinguished member of the Asteraceae family. Standing about 30 to 60 cm tall, the plant showcases lance-shaped leaves and striking orange to yellow flower heads, blooming from early spring through late autumn. The daisy-like flowers can reach up to 4 inches in diameter, with multiple layers of petals encircling a central disk.

Known Hazards: Those who are allergic to plants in the Asteraceae family should proceed with caution. It's also not recommended during pregnancy or breastfeeding.

Habitats: Calendula officinalis prefers well-drained soil and a sunny location but is fairly adaptable to less-than-ideal conditions, including poor, sandy soil and partial shade.

Range: Originally native to Southern Europe, it is now cultivated widely around the world and naturalized in many areas.

Identification: Calendula officinalis is easily identified by its vivid, orange or yellow, daisy-like flower heads that are comprised of ray and disc florets. The leaves are lance-shaped, and the plant itself exudes a sticky, resinous feel.

Edible Uses: The petals are edible and can be used fresh to add a burst of color to salads, or dried for later use. They offer a slightly tangy, peppery taste. The petals are also a popular substitute for saffron in cooking.

Medicinal Uses: Calendula has a long-standing reputation in traditional medicine for its anti-inflammatory, antifungal, and antibacterial properties. The flowers are commonly used to make tinctures, ointments, and teas for a variety of skin ailments including burns, cuts, and rashes. The anti-inflammatory properties extend to internal use, as the plant has been employed to treat minor digestive and oral issues. Always consult healthcare professionals before considering any plant for medicinal uses.

Other Uses: It can be used to make natural dyes.

Caltha palustris

Common Name: Marsh Marigold, Kingcup

Family: Ranunculaceae

Description: The Marsh Marigold, or Kingcup, is a perennial herbaceous plant recognized for its glistening yellow flowers. Preferring wet environments like fens, marshes, and stream margins, the plant typically grows in clumps with stems reaching up to 60 cm in height. Its shiny, dark green leaves, often heart-shaped to kidney-shaped, complement its vivid blossoms. Blooming from early spring to mid-summer, the flowers are large, usually around 2-5 cm in diameter, with five to nine petal-like sepals that radiate a sunny allure. The plant plays an essential role in early spring as a nectar source for pollinators.

Known Hazards: While all parts of the Marsh Marigold are poisonous when consumed raw due to the presence of protoanemonin, the toxin can be neutralized by drying or cooking. The sap may also irritate sensitive skin.

Habitats: Marsh Marigold thrives in wet and boggy conditions. They are frequently found near ponds, streams, marshes, fens, and wet woodlands.

Range: This plant is native to temperate regions of the Northern Hemisphere, covering parts of North America, Europe, and Asia.

Identification: To identify Caltha palustris, one should look for its iconic, glossy yellow flowers, which give the appearance of being a type of buttercup. The flowers sit atop hollow stems and consist of petal-like sepals as they lack true petals. The leaves are generally large, succulent, and heart or kidney-shaped, with a smooth edge, sometimes exhibiting a slightly serrated margin. The leaves at the base are often larger and on long stalks, while those higher up the stem may be more sessile and smaller. These features, combined with its favored wet habitat, make the Marsh Marigold distinguishable from many other wildflowers.

Edible Uses: The flower buds, when pickled, can be a substitute for capers. However, they must be boiled first and then soaked in a brine or vinegar solution. Older leaves, after thorough boiling, can also be eaten as they lose their toxic properties, but the flavor is quite strong and might not appeal to everyone.

Medicinal Uses: Historically, Marsh Marigold has been used for medicinal purposes, such as an expectorant or diuretic, and to treat warts. However, due to its potential toxicity, internal use, especially without expert guidance, is not recommended.

Other Uses: The bright yellow flowers of the Marsh Marigold have been used to make dyes, producing colors ranging from yellow to green.

Chenopodium album

Common Name: Lamb's Quarters, Fat-hen, Goosefoot, White Goosefoot

Family: Amaranthaceae

Description: The plant typically grows up to 1 to 2 meters in height and is characterized by its triangular to diamond-shaped leaves. The plant produces tiny greenish flowers in dense, spike-like clusters from late spring to late summer.

Known Hazards: Though generally considered safe to eat, consumption in large quantities may lead to digestive issues due to its oxalate content. Also, it is crucial to ensure that the plant has not been exposed to herbicides or pollutants.

Habitats: Chenopodium album thrives in a variety of soil conditions but prefers nitrogen-rich, well-drained soils. It is commonly found in disturbed sites like roadsides, fields, and waste areas.

Range: This species is cosmopolitan in distribution, found across all continents except Antarctica. It is particularly prevalent in North America, Europe, and Asia.

Identification: The plant is distinguished by its mealy appearance, with a whitish coating on the leaves and stems. The leaves are alternate, and their shape ranges from lanceolate to broadly rhombic. Flowers are minute and green, clustered at the tips of branches in a spike-like arrangement.

Edible Uses: The young leaves are edible and can be consumed either raw or cooked. They make an excellent addition to salads and can be cooked like spinach. The seeds are also edible and can be ground into flour or used as a quinoa substitute.

Medicinal Uses: In traditional medicine, Chenopodium album has been used for its antiseptic, digestive, and anti-inflammatory properties. It is believed to be beneficial for treating gastrointestinal issues like dyspepsia and has been used topically for skin conditions.

Cirsium edule

Family: Asteraceae

Description: With spiny, lance-shaped leaves and a thick stem, this thistle can reach a height of up to 2 meters. It showcases a prominent flowering head that usually consists of vibrant purple or lavender flowers. The blooming period typically spans from late spring to early summer.

Known Hazards: Although the plant is largely considered safe for consumption, caution is advised due to the spiny leaves and stems, which can cause physical discomfort upon handling.

Habitats: The plant favors well-drained but moist soils and thrives in open, sunny fields, meadows, and along forest edges. It is often found in both lowlands and mountainous regions.

Range: Native to the western regions of North America, its natural habitat stretches from Alaska down through British Columbia to Oregon and eastwards into Montana.

Identification: Cirsium edule is characterized by its spiny leaves, which are deeply lobed and have a somewhat woolly texture on the underside. The plant typically has a single, thick, hairy stem that may branch near the top. The vibrant purple or lavender flower heads are the most conspicuous feature, usually appearing in solitary or clustered formations at the tips of stems.

Edible Uses: The root, young shoots, and the inner portion of young stems are edible and have a mildly sweet, nutty flavor. They can be consumed raw or cooked and are often used in stews and stir-fries. The young leaves, after removal of spines, can be cooked and consumed as a leafy vegetable.

Medicinal Uses: Though not extensively documented, the plant has been traditionally used for its anti-inflammatory properties, particularly in the treatment of digestive and skin disorders. The roots have been used as a tonic and to stimulate appetite.

Claytonia perfoliata

Common Name: Miner's Lettuce, Indian Lettuce

Family: Montiaceae

Description: This plant typically grows to a height of about 5-40 cm, forming a basal rosette of leaves. During its blooming period from late winter to spring, it bears small, white to light pink flowers that emerge from a unique, perforated, disk-like bract, which lends the plant its scientific name.

Habitats: Native to western North America, this plant prefers moist, shaded locations. It is often found in woodlands, alongside streams, and in other damp areas where the soil is well-drained but retains moisture.

Range: This plant is most commonly found in the western regions of North America, from Alaska and British Columbia down to Central California. It has also naturalized in some parts of the eastern United States.

Identification: Miner's Lettuce can be identified by its fleshy, spoon-shaped leaves that form a basal rosette. The stem is often succulent, and the unique disk-like bract that encircles the stem is a distinguishing feature. The small, five-petaled flowers appear to sprout directly from this perforated bract, usually in clusters.

Edible Uses: The young leaves of Claytonia perforata are edible and can be consumed raw or cooked. They have a crisp texture and a mild, slightly sweet flavor, making them an excellent addition to salads or as a garnish.

Medicinal Uses: The leaves are rich in Vitamin C and were historically consumed by Native American tribes to prevent scurvy.

Crataegus monogyna

Common Name: Common Hawthorn, Single-seeded Hawthorn, Mayblossom

Family: Rosaceae

Description: Crataegus monogyna, commonly known as Common Hawthorn, is a small to medium-sized deciduous tree in the Rosaceae family. This robust tree can grow up to 15 meters in height, with a spread nearly as wide. It's recognized for its dense crown and thorny branches. Its small, deeply lobed leaves adorn the branches, providing a lush green backdrop for the abundant white or pinkish flowers that bloom in late spring. By late summer to early autumn, the flowers give way to red berries known as haws.

Known Hazards: The seeds within the haws contain cyanogenic glycosides and should not be consumed. Also, people with heart conditions should consult a healthcare professional before using Hawthorn medicinally.

Habitats: Prefers a variety of soil types but thrives in well-drained soil. It is often found in hedgerows, woodland edges, and open fields.

Range: Native to Europe, North Africa, and West Asia, it has also been naturalized in other parts of the world, including North America.

Identification: One of the most prominent features that sets Crataegus monogyna apart is its thorny branches, which are often dark brown to black and densely packed to form a hedge-like structure. Examine the leaves closely, and you'll find them to be deeply lobed—usually with 3-5 lobes—and approximately 2-4 cm in length. Their texture can be described as somewhat leathery, with a glossy appearance on the upper side. During late spring, the tree is bedecked with small, 5-petaled white or slightly pinkish flowers that grow in dense corymbs or clusters. A discerning characteristic is the scent of the flowers, which some describe as unpleasant or fish-like, but it's this feature that could prevent you from mistaking it for other similar flowering trees. By late summer to early autumn, these flowers give way to red berries known as haws. Unlike many other species in the Crataegus genus, the haws of Crataegus monogyna contain only a single seed, which is an important detail in distinguishing it from other hawthorns. The haws are usually about 1 cm in diameter and may have a slightly flattened shape.

Edible Uses: The haws are edible but bland, often used to make jellies, jams, and even wine. However, care must be taken to remove the seeds.

Medicinal Uses: The berries, leaves, and flowers of Crataegus monogyna have been used for centuries for their cardiovascular benefits. They are believed to improve heart health, reduce symptoms of heart failure, and help regulate blood pressure. In traditional medicine, the plant has also been employed as a digestive aid and anxiety reliever. However, it's crucial to consult healthcare professionals before using this plant for medicinal purposes.

Elaeagnus umbellata

Common Name: Autumn Olive, Japanese Silverberry, Umbellata Oleaster

Family: Elaeagnaceae

Description: Elaeagnus umbellata, commonly known as Autumn Olive or Japanese Silverberry, is a deciduous shrub or tree that can reach up to 6 meters in height. It bears simple, alternate leaves with a silvery underside. Clusters of fragrant, tubular, cream-colored to pale yellow flowers bloom in late spring to early summer, attracting pollinators. By late summer to early autumn, the shrub produces an abundance of small, red or amber berries speckled with silver.

Known Hazards: While the berries are edible, consumption should be moderate due to their high sugar content.

Habitats: This adaptable plant thrives in a variety of conditions but particularly favors well-drained, sandy to loamy soils. It is often found in open woodlands, fields, and disturbed areas.

Range: Originally native to Asia, Elaeagnus umbellata has been naturalized in various parts of Europe and North America.

Identification: To correctly identify Elaeagnus umbellata, start by observing the leaves. These are simple and alternate, but what sets them apart is the silvery scale-like dots present on the underside, which give it a distinctive silvery appearance. The edges of the leaves are smooth, and they lack any form of serration. Next, pay attention to the plant's blooming period between late spring and early summer. The flowers are tubular and range in color from cream to pale yellow; these flowers emit a strong, sweet fragrance. Come late summer to early autumn, clusters of berries begin to appear. These are small, ranging between 4-9 mm, and their color varies from red to amber. A notable characteristic is the presence of silver speckles on these berries.

Edible Uses: The berries are not only edible but also high in vitamin C and antioxidants. They can be consumed fresh or used in making jams, jellies, and sauces.

Other Uses: The fragrant flowers can be used in potpourri.

Fragaria virginiana

Common Name: Wild Strawberry, Virginia Strawberry

Family: Rosaceae

Description: Fragaria virginiana, or the Wild Strawberry, is a low-growing perennial that reaches only about 15 to 30 cm in height. It forms dense mats via runners. Its trifoliate leaves are dark green, coarsely toothed, and typically hairy underneath. The plant boasts small, white, five-petaled flowers that appear in late spring and transform into bright red, juicy berries by early to mid-summer. These diminutive fruits are replete with seeds on their surface.

Known Hazards: No serious hazards are associated with the consumption of this plant, although caution is advised for those allergic to strawberries.

Habitats: The Wild Strawberry prefers well-drained, sandy to loamy soils and is often found in open fields, meadows, and woodland edges.

Range: Native to North America, its range spans from the eastern U.S. to the Rocky Mountains and northwards into Canada.

Identification: Distinctive trifoliate leaves and the presence of small, white, five-petaled flowers transitioning into tiny, red strawberries are telltale identification markers for this plant.

Edible Uses: The berries are delicious and can be eaten fresh or used in culinary preparations like jams, jellies, and desserts. The leaves are sometimes used to make a mild, strawberry-flavored tea.

Medicinal Uses: Traditionally, the leaves of Fragaria virginiana have been used to make teas that are rich in tannins, and are considered to possess mild astringent and diuretic properties. However, its medicinal uses are not as pronounced as some other plants, and one should consult a healthcare professional for any medicinal applications.

Other Uses: It can be used for dyeing fabrics a yellow-green color.

Hemerocallis fulva

Common Name: Orange Daylily, Tawny Daylily, Tiger Daylily

Family: Hemerocallidaceae

Description: This plant, native to Asia but widely naturalized in North America, can grow up to 1.2 meters in height. It is characterized by its vibrant, trumpet-shaped orange flowers that bloom from late spring to early summer. Each flower lasts only one day, giving the plant its name, "Daylily." It thrives in full sun to partial shade and is remarkably hardy, tolerating various soil conditions.

Known Hazards: While the plant is largely considered edible, it is advisable to proceed with caution as it could cause mild stomach upset in some individuals. Ensure proper identification before consumption.

Habitats: Hemerocallis fulva prefers well-drained, moderately fertile soil but is highly adaptable to various conditions. It is often found in meadows, along roadsides, and even in urban environments, where it is frequently used for ornamental purposes.

Range: Though originally from Asia, the Orange Daylily has naturalized widely across Europe and North America, particularly in the eastern and central regions of the United States and Canada.

Identification: The Orange Daylily has lanceolate leaves that form a dense clump at the base of the plant. The leaves are typically 50-90 cm long and 1-2.5 cm wide, arching gracefully toward the ground. The flower stalks rise above the foliage, each carrying multiple buds that bloom into large, six-petaled orange flowers with a darker orange or red interior. Each flower is 7–10 cm across and consists of three inner petals and three outer sepals, all of which are usually the same color.

Edible Uses: The young green leaves, flower buds, and tuberous roots of Hemerocallis fulva are edible. They can be consumed raw in salads or cooked in various dishes. The flower buds can be stir-fried, steamed, or used in soups. The roots are starchy and can be boiled or roasted.

Medicinal Uses: In traditional medicine, the plant has been used to treat various ailments including urinary disorders, menstrual irregularities, and insomnia. However, scientific evidence supporting these claims is limited.

Hydrophyllum virginianum

Common Name: Virginia Waterleaf

Family: Boraginaceae

Description: Hydrophyllum virginianum, or Virginia Waterleaf, is a perennial herb known for its distinctive foliage and showy flowers. It is native to the eastern regions of North America. The plant can grow between 30 to 60 cm tall, showcasing a mound-like growth habit with a sprawling nature, making it a popular choice for woodland gardens.

Habitats: Virginia Waterleaf prefers shaded woodlands, rich moist woods, and thickets. It flourishes particularly well in areas with dappled sunlight and well-drained, humus-rich soils.

Range: The plant is naturally found across the eastern regions of North America, from Quebec to Manitoba in Canada, and stretching southwards to Texas and Florida in the United States.

Identification: Virginia Waterleaf's most distinctive characteristic is its foliage. The leaves are large, lobed, and bear a certain resemblance to maple leaves. They are typically light green, often marked with white or pale blotches that look like water spots, giving the plant its common name. The flowers of Virginia Waterleaf are bell-shaped and generally lavender or pale blue, though occasionally they may also be white. These flowers appear in clusters on hairy stalks that rise above the foliage, typically in late spring to early summer. The plant's stems are often covered with fine hairs and may take on a reddish hue as they mature.

Edible Uses: The young leaves and shoots of the plant can be consumed either raw or cooked. When eaten raw, they are often added to salads, while when cooked, they can be used much like spinach. The leaves have a mild, pleasant flavor.

Medicinal Uses: Traditionally, Native American tribes used Hydrophyllum virginianum for various medicinal purposes, including as a poultice for wounds and as a treatment for stomach disorders. However, there's limited contemporary evidence supporting these traditional uses.

Juglans cinerea

Common Name: Butternut, White Walnut

Family: Juglandaceae

Description: The Butternut, colloquially known as White Walnut, is a deciduous tree endemic to the Juglandaceae family. Revered for its stately presence, the Butternut can reach up to 30 meters in height. It has pinnately compound leaves with a distinctive, elongated terminal leaflet. Its bark is smooth and grayish, gradually becoming ridged as the tree matures. In early summer, the tree bursts into greenish-yellow catkins which eventually produce oblong, husked fruits encapsulating the edible nuts.

Known Hazards: The nut, when consumed in excessive amounts, might cause gastrointestinal distress for some.

Habitats: Butternut trees prefer well-draining soils and are commonly found in river valleys, woodlands, and near streams. They thrive in areas with full sun but can tolerate light shade.

Range: Native to the eastern United States and southeast Canada, the Butternut has, however, experienced significant decline in certain regions due to the Butternut canker disease.

Identification: To identify a Butternut tree, one can look for distinctive clues: its oblong, sticky, husked fruits which house the edible nut, the pinnately compound leaves which often have an elongated terminal leaflet, and its gray, furrowed bark that emits a yellow tint when scratched. The nuts themselves are elongated and feature a rough, hard shell.

Edible Uses: The nut inside the fruit husk is the primary edible component of the Butternut tree. They have a rich, buttery flavor, thus earning the tree its name. The nuts can be consumed raw, roasted, or incorporated into a variety of dishes. Additionally, the sap from the tree can be tapped and boiled down to produce syrup, much like maple syrup.

Medicinal Uses: Historically, the inner bark of the Butternut tree was used by indigenous populations as a laxative. It's also been employed for its potential anti-inflammatory and tonic properties. However, as with all medicinal uses, it's crucial to consult with a health professional before use.

Other Uses: The husks and bark were traditionally used as a source of yellowish-brown dye.

Laportea canadensis

Common Name: Canadian Wood Nettle, Wood Nettle

Family: Urticaceae

Description: Laportea canadensis, or the Canadian Wood Nettle, is a perennial herbaceous plant native to North America. Recognized by its toothed leaves and clustered greenish flowers, it prefers the rich, moist soils of woodlands and is commonly found along streams or in shaded clearings. Despite being a nettle, it is not as stinging as its close relative, the stinging nettle (Urtica dioica), but can still cause mild skin irritation.

Known Hazards: The hairs on the leaves and stems of the wood nettle contain a stinging substance that can cause irritation when touched. While the sensation is usually mild and short-lived, it is advisable to handle the plant with care or wear gloves.

Habitats: Prefers rich, moist soils commonly found in woodlands, floodplains, and along stream banks. It thrives in shaded or partially shaded areas.

Range: Primarily found in the Eastern and Central parts of North America.

Identification: When identifying the Canadian Wood Nettle, look for its distinct opposite leaves with coarse teeth. The leaves and stem will have stinging hairs, although they are less potent than those of the stinging nettle. The greenish-white flowers are not particularly showy and grow in clusters. The plant has a robust, erect growth habit and can often form dense colonies in suitable habitats.

Edible Uses: The young shoots and leaves of the wood nettle can be cooked and consumed, much like spinach, after boiling them in two changes of water to remove the stinging properties. They offer a rich, green flavor and are high in vitamins and minerals. The seeds can also be eaten either raw or cooked.

Medicinal Uses: Traditionally, the Canadian Wood Nettle has been used in native herbal medicine to treat various ailments. A poultice of the plant was used to relieve sore muscles, and an infusion was consumed to help with internal problems like stomachaches.

Other Uses: Nets, cordage

Matteuccia struthiopteris

Common Name: Ostrich Fern

Family: Onocleaceae

Description: The Ostrich Fern is a strikingly tall and elegant perennial fern, named for its large, feather-like fronds that are reminiscent of ostrich plumes. This fern can grow up to 1.5 to 2 meters in height. The fronds emerge in a tight, upright clump and then gracefully arch outward. The plant produces separate fertile and sterile fronds. The sterile fronds are the large, showy green ones, while the fertile fronds are smaller, brown, and more rigid.

Known Hazards: The ostrich fern is primarily safe for consumption, especially the young fiddleheads. However, there are other ferns with similar-looking young fiddleheads that can be toxic. The Bracken Fern, for instance, which is considered carcinogenic, might be confused with the Ostrich Fern. To correctly identify the Ostrich Fern fiddlehead, look for a deep U-shaped groove on the inside of the main stem. The base of the fern will also have brown, papery scales.

Habitats: Ostrich ferns prefer shaded or semi-shaded areas, typically flourishing in damp woodlands, riverbanks, and other moist, fertile soils.

Range: Native to the northern hemisphere, the Ostrich Fern is found throughout Canada and the northern United States. Its range also stretches across Eurasia.

Identification: Ostrich Ferns are recognized for their dimorphic fronds. Sterile fronds are bright green, tall, and arch gracefully, resembling ostrich plumes. In contrast, fertile fronds are shorter, brown, and stand upright. These fertile fronds persist through the winter. The base of the fern, where the fiddlehead emerges, is covered in a brown, papery scale. When trying to identify this fern, it's essential to note the deep U-shaped groove on the inside of the main stem (or stipe).

Edible Uses: Raw or undercooked fiddleheads of the Ostrich Fern can contain microbes or toxins that can lead to foodborne illnesses. Symptoms might include nausea, vomiting, and diarrhea. Always ensure that fiddleheads are cooked thoroughly—boiled for at least 15 minutes or steamed for 10-12 minutes—before consumption. They should not be eaten raw or lightly sautéed. While the young fiddleheads are edible, the mature fronds or older parts of the Ostrich Fern are not typically consumed, as they can be tough and might cause stomach discomfort.

Monarda didyma

Common Name: Scarlet Bee Balm, Oswego Tea, Bergamot

Family: Lamiaceae

Description: Monarda didyma, commonly known as Scarlet Bee Balm, is a perennial herb that reaches heights of 90 to 120 cm. The plant is easily identified by its vibrant, scarlet-red tubular flowers, which form in dense, rounded clusters at the top of the stems. The leaves are lanceolate to ovate, with a rich green hue, and are often tinged with a reddish or purplish hue. The plant has a strong minty aroma and is especially attractive to pollinators like bees and hummingbirds.

Known Hazards: Generally considered safe, but those with sensitivities to plants in the mint family should exercise caution.

Habitats: Scarlet Bee Balm thrives in rich, well-drained soil and prefers full sun to partial shade. It is frequently found in moist meadows, woodland clearings, and along riverbanks.

Range: Native to eastern North America, it ranges from Ontario and Quebec down to Georgia and westward as far as Minnesota.

Identification: Look for the characteristic scarlet-red flower clusters, which resemble a fireworks display, and lanceolate, aromatic leaves. When crushed, the leaves release a strong, minty scent.

Edible Uses: The young leaves and flower petals can be used to make teas, salads, and garnishes. Their minty flavor adds a unique twist to culinary creations.

Medicinal Uses: Monarda didyma has been traditionally used for its antiseptic properties. A tea made from its leaves has been employed for treating digestive issues, sore throats, and colds. The plant contains thymol, which is a potent antiseptic and the active ingredient in many commercial mouthwashes. Always consult a healthcare provider before using the plant for medicinal purposes.

Other Uses: Its aromatic leaves can also serve as an insect repellent when crushed and rubbed onto the skin.

Nasturtium officinale

Common Name: Watercress

Family: Brassicaceae

Description: Nasturtium officinale, or Watercress, is a perennial aquatic or semi-aquatic herb, characterized by its small, white, four-petaled flowers and pinnately compound leaves. The plant tends to form lush, aquatic mats that float on the water's surface, with stems reaching lengths of 50 to 60 cm. It's a popular ingredient in salads due to its peppery flavor.

Known Hazards: Consuming large quantities may lead to stomach upset. The plant has the potential to accumulate harmful water-borne parasites and bacteria, so it's critical to source it from clean, uncontaminated water.

Habitats: Watercress typically grows in slow-moving or stagnant water bodies like streams, rivers, and ponds, often fully or partially submerged.

Range: Native to Europe and Asia but has been naturalized worldwide, including North America.

Identification: Look for the glossy, green, pinnately compound leaves that have a peppery scent when crushed. The white flowers with four petals are also a giveaway.

Edible Uses: Watercress is commonly used in salads, sandwiches, and as a garnish. It's a popular component in soups and can also be sautéed or used in stir-fries. Due to its peppery taste, it adds a zest to various dishes.

Medicinal Uses: Watercress has been used traditionally as a diuretic and expectorant. It's rich in vitamins A, C, and K, as well as other essential nutrients. It has been suggested to have cancer-fighting properties due to its high phytonutrient content. However, consult a healthcare provider for medicinal applications.

Oenothera biennis

Common Name: Evening Primrose, Common Evening Primrose, Evening Star

Family: Onagraceae

Description: Oenothera biennis, the Evening Primrose, is a biennial flowering plant. In the first year, it forms a rosette of leaves at ground level; during the second year, it sends up a spike up to 1.5 meters tall, bearing bright yellow flowers that open late in the day, hence the name. These blooms are followed by elongated seed capsules. The plant is well-known for its medicinal properties and the oil derived from its seeds.

Known Hazards: While generally considered safe for consumption, some people might experience side effects such as stomach upset or headaches. It's also noted that people with epilepsy or those prone to seizures should avoid using Evening Primrose due to the potential of inducing seizures.

Habitats: This plant thrives in sunny and well-drained habitats. It's commonly found in disturbed soils, fields, roadsides, and wastelands.

Range: Native to North America, Evening Primrose has since been introduced to Europe and parts of Asia. It is found across most of the United States and Canada.

Identification: Aside from its bright yellow, four-petaled flowers that open in the evening, one of the defining characteristics of the Evening Primrose is its long seed pods. Another notable feature is the plant's biennial growth pattern.

Edible Uses: The roots are edible and can be boiled like potatoes. Young seedpods can be cooked and consumed, and the young leaves are often added to salads. The seeds are a source of Evening Primrose oil, which is used both culinarily and medicinally.

Medicinal Uses: Evening Primrose oil, extracted from the seeds, is rich in gamma-linolenic acid (GLA) and is used for various ailments, including eczema, premenstrual syndrome, and arthritis. Traditional uses also include the treatment of asthma, gastrointestinal complaints, and as a sedative.

Opuntia spp.

Common Name: Prickly Pear, Nopal

Family: Cactaceae

Description: Belonging to the cactus family, Opuntia spp., commonly known as prickly pear or nopal, is a genus of flowering plants native to the Americas but have also adapted to various climates around the world. These plants exhibit a unique, segmented structure made up of flat, fleshy pads known as "cladodes." The pads sprout spiky thorns and are crowned with bright yellow, red, or purple flowers that bloom from late spring into summer. Following the flowering stage, the plants produce edible fruit known as "tunas."

Known Hazards: The plant is covered in sharp spines, as well as smaller, hair-like glochids that are difficult to see and remove. These can cause skin irritation or injury if not handled carefully.

Habitat: Opuntia spp. are highly adaptable and can grow in a variety of environments but are primarily found in arid and semi-arid regions.

Range: Native to the Americas, these species have naturalized in various parts of the world, from the United States to Africa, Australia, and the Mediterranean.

Identification: To identify an Opuntia, one looks for the distinct flat, fleshy, green to bluish-green pads with tufts of spines or glochids at regular intervals. The flowers are often large and showy, ranging in color from yellow to red or purple. Following the flowering stage, the fruits are also fairly easy to identify: rounded and often covered in small spines, they range from green to reddish-purple when ripe.

Edible Uses: Both the young cladodes and the fruit are edible. The pads are often cooked and used in dishes like salads and stews, while the fruits can be eaten fresh or used to make jellies and beverages. Seeds within the fruit are also edible but are often discarded due to their hard texture.

Medicinal Uses: Traditionally, Opuntia spp. have been used for a variety of medicinal purposes, including the treatment of burns, wounds, and digestive issues. Recent research suggests they may have anti-inflammatory, antiviral, and antidiabetic properties, although more studies are needed to confirm these effects.

Other Uses: The mucilaginous liquid found inside the cladodes has been used as a hair conditioner and in the making of cosmetics. In some regions, the thorny pads are used as natural fencing to deter predators.

Oxalis acetosella

Common Name: Wood Sorrel, Common Wood Sorrel

Family: Oxalidaceae

Description: Oxalis acetosella, commonly known as Wood Sorrel, is a perennial herb distinguished by its trifoliate leaves resembling clover. The plant grows up to 15 cm in height and prefers shaded, moist forested areas. The delicate white or light pink flowers bloom from spring through summer, often closing up at night or during cloudy weather.

Known Hazards: Consumption in large quantities can lead to oxalate poisoning, causing symptoms like nausea and calcium deficiency. It should be avoided by individuals with kidney problems or gout.

Habitats: Wood Sorrel is typically found in moist, shaded woodlands and forested areas.

Range: It is native to much of Europe and Asia, though it has been introduced elsewhere.

Identification: To identify Oxalis acetosella, look for trifoliate leaves with distinct heart-shaped leaflets that are often folded through the middle. The plant's flowers are usually white or pale pink with five petals and may feature delicate pink streaks. Unique to this species is the leaves' subtle folding and the flowers' tendency to close during nighttime or overcast conditions. These detailed features make Oxalis acetosella easily distinguishable, allowing for confident identification.

Edible Uses: The leaves have a lemony, tangy taste and can be used in small quantities to flavor salads, sauces, and stews. The flowers are also edible and can add a decorative touch to dishes.

Medicinal Uses: Traditionally, wood sorrel has been used for its astringent and diuretic properties. A poultice of the leaves can be applied to skin irritations and wounds for relief. Infusions have been used to treat fevers and urinary infections.

Pastinaca sativa

Common Name: Wild Parsnip

Family: Apiaceae

Description: Wild Parsnip is a biennial plant characterized by its rosette of pinnate, hairy leaves and a cream-colored, tapering taproot. In the first year, the plant focuses on root development. Come the second year, it sends up a flowering stalk, up to 1.5 meters high, crowned with yellow umbelliferous flowers.

Known Hazards: Wild Parsnip's sap can induce phytophotodermatitis, causing skin irritation and possibly long-lasting discoloration when exposed to sunlight. Consuming the root of wild parsnip may cause oral irritation or allergic reactions in some individuals.

Habitats: Thrives in full sun, fertile, well-drained soils; commonly found in fields, pastures, and roadsides.

Range: Originating from Eurasia, wild parsnip is now widespread in North America.

Identification: Wild Parsnip can be identified by its pinnate leaves with broad leaflets, somewhat hairy in texture. The root is cream-colored and tapered, resembling a carrot. Yellow flowers are arranged in umbels during its second year. One of the distinguishing features of edible wild Pastinaca sativa is its slightly hairy leaves and cream-colored roots. It's crucial to differentiate it from other, often toxic, Apiaceae species like Water Hemlock or Poison Hemlock, which can have smooth leaves and different root structures.

Edible Uses: The cream-colored root is the primary edible part and has a sweet, nutty flavor when cooked. It can be roasted, boiled, or mashed.

Medicinal Uses: Historically, the seeds were used for their diuretic and emmenagogue properties. The root has been applied as a poultice for inflammations and sores.

Portulaca oleracea sativa

Common Name: Purslane, Garden Purslane

Family: Portulacaceae

Description: Portulaca oleracea sativa, commonly known as garden purslane, is an annual herb that is a cultivated variant of the wild purslane. Renowned for its fleshy, succulent leaves and stems, it's a heat-loving plant that grows close to the ground in a sprawling manner. It can reach up to 30 cm in height. Yellow, star-shaped flowers adorn the plant but often open only in full sunlight.

Known Hazards: While generally safe to consume, it's important to note that it contains oxalic acid, which could be a concern for individuals prone to kidney stones.

Habitats: Thriving in well-drained soils, it prefers sunny locations and is drought-tolerant. It is a versatile plant that can grow in a variety of settings, from gardens to disturbed lands.

Range: Originating in the Middle East, it has been widely cultivated and naturalized globally.

Identification: The fleshy leaves are paddle-shaped and vibrant green, contrasting sharply with the red or green stems. Yellow, five-petaled flowers are generally about 6 mm in diameter and only open during intense sunlight, making them an essential identification marker. The plants have a sprawling growth habit, often forming mats over the soil.

Edible Uses: Purslane leaves and stems are edible both raw and cooked. They possess a slightly tangy flavor and are often added to salads, stews, or stir-fries. The seeds can also be ground into a meal.

Medicinal Uses: Rich in omega-3 fatty acids and antioxidants, purslane has anti-inflammatory properties. It's used traditionally to treat conditions like arthritis and asthma.

Prosopis juliflora

Common Name: Mesquite, Algarrobo, Bayahonda, Jumbie Bean

Family: Fabaceae

Description: Prosopis juliflora, commonly known as mesquite, is a deciduous tree or shrub belonging to the legume family. It can grow from 3 to 12 meters in height, depending on the environment. This highly adaptable plant is known for its drought tolerance and can flourish in arid conditions. It produces small, yellow-green flowers, which give way to long, slender, bean-like pods.

Known Hazards: When collecting, pay attention to spines or sharp edges.

Habitats: Mesquite is highly adaptable but predominantly thrives in arid and semi-arid regions with well-drained soils.

Range: Native to the Americas, it has been widely introduced to parts of Africa, Asia, and Australia, where it can sometimes become invasive.

Identification: The leaves are bipinnate, featuring tiny leaflets that are bright green and slightly feathery to the touch. The yellow-green flowers appear in spike-like clusters and are mildly fragrant. The distinctive bean-like pods are straight or slightly curved, varying in length but generally around 20 cm. These pods change from green to a mature, dark brown color as they age.

Edible Uses: The pods can be ground into a flour that is used in breads and cakes. The seeds are also edible and can be roasted or boiled.

Medicinal Uses: In traditional medicine, mesquite bark has been used for treating skin conditions and digestive issues. The leaves have been employed for their antiseptic properties.

Other Uses: The pods have been used as a natural dye.

Prunus pensylvanica

Common Name: Pin Cherry, Fire Cherry, Wild Red Cherry

Family: Rosaceae

Description: The Pin Cherry, also commonly known as the Fire Cherry or Wild Red Cherry, is a small deciduous tree in the Rosaceae family. This tree, characterized by its slender form, usually grows between 6 to 12 meters in height. It is primarily recognized for its bright red cherries and its smooth, reddish-brown bark that peels horizontally. Blossoming in the late spring, the tree showcases delicate white flowers that later transition to vibrant cherries by mid-summer.

Known Hazards: The leaves, twigs, and seeds of the Pin Cherry contain hydrocyanic acid, which is toxic when ingested in large quantities. Although the flesh of the cherries is safe to consume, care should be taken to avoid ingesting the seeds.

Habitats: Pin Cherry thrives in well-drained soils and can often be found in clearings, burned areas, and forest edges. It's a pioneering species that often dominates landscapes following disturbances, setting the stage for longer-lived tree species to take over.

Range: This tree is native to North America, with a range stretching from the eastern to the central parts of the continent. Its presence is significant from Newfoundland to the Dakotas and extends southward to the mountainous regions of Georgia and Tennessee.

Identification: Distinguishing the Pin Cherry is made simpler by observing its smooth, reddish-brown bark that often peels off in horizontal strips. Its leaves are lanceolate to oblong and finely serrated at the edges, exhibiting a lustrous green hue. During its flowering phase, it presents clusters of small, white flowers. By mid-summer, these flowers give way to bright red cherries, each containing a single seed. These cherries, while sour when raw, can be identified by their bright coloration and shiny appearance.

Edible Uses: The cherries of the Prunus pensylvanica, though quite tart when consumed raw, can be used in jams, jellies, and pies. They can also be dried for later use. When preparing these fruits for consumption, it's essential to ensure the removal of the seeds due to their toxic nature.

Medicinal Uses: Historically, Native American tribes used parts of the Pin Cherry tree for medicinal purposes. The bark, when boiled, was used to make teas and decoctions for treating colds, coughs, and diarrhea. However, it's crucial to note that modern use should be approached with caution due to the inherent toxicity in some parts of the tree.

Prunus virginiana

Common Name: Chokecherry

Family: Rosaceae

Description: Prunus virginiana, popularly known as Chokecherry, is a deciduous shrub or tree that belongs to the Rosaceae family. It typically grows to heights between 3 to 8 meters. This plant features shiny, oblong leaves and produces racemes of fragrant white flowers in the late spring. By late summer, these flowers give way to clusters of small, dark red to black cherries.

Known Hazards: The seeds, leaves, and twigs of the Chokecherry contain hydrocyanic acid, which is toxic when ingested. While the flesh of the fruit is edible, care should be taken to avoid consuming large quantities of the seeds. Cooking can reduce the cyanogenic glycosides present in the fruit, but the seeds should always be discarded.

Habitats: Prunus virginiana prefers sunny to partially shaded areas. It thrives in well-drained soils and is commonly found in woodlands, thickets, and along streambanks and roadsides.

Range: This plant is native to North America and can be found throughout most of the United States and Canada, from the Atlantic to the Pacific.

Identification: To identify Prunus virginiana, look for its clusters of white flowers in spring, followed by the appearance of dark cherries in late summer. The leaves are typically bright green on top and lighter underneath.

Edible Uses: The fruit from the Chokecherry is edible and is commonly used to make jellies, jams, wines, and syrups. While the raw cherries are astringent, cooking or processing it, especially with the addition of sugar, makes it more palatable. Remember always to discard the seeds when consuming or processing.

Medicinal Uses: Historically, various Native American tribes used parts of the Chokecherry plant for medicinal purposes. The bark, when properly prepared, was used to treat conditions like diarrhea, coughs, and tuberculosis. However, due to the plant's inherent toxicity, it's essential to use it medicinally only under the guidance of a knowledgeable healthcare professional.

Rhus spp.

Common Names: Sumac, Smooth Sumac, Staghorn Sumac, Poison Sumac, and others depending on the specific species

Family: Anacardiaceae

Description: The Rhus genus comprises both shrubs and small trees. They are characterized by their pinnately compound leaves, which can turn brilliant shades of red, orange, and purple in the fall. Many species bear dense conical clusters of small flowers, which give way to clusters of bright red berries in late summer and autumn.

Known Hazards: While many species of Rhus are harmless and even beneficial, the genus includes Poison Sumac (Rhus vernix), which contains urushiol, an oil that can cause severe allergic dermatitis upon contact. The reaction is similar to that caused by poison ivy and poison oak. It's crucial to differentiate between the harmless and toxic species of this genus.

Habitats: Sumacs are often found in open, sunny areas. They can thrive in various habitats from roadsides, forest edges, and pastures to disturbed areas where they might grow as opportunistic pioneers.

Range: The Rhus species have a wide distribution across North America, with certain species also found in parts of Africa, Asia, and Europe.

Identification: Sumacs are identifiable by their fern-like leaves and the typical red berry clusters present in many species. The branches of Staghorn Sumac (Rhus typhina) are covered in fine hairs, giving them the appearance of a stag's antlers in velvet. In contrast, Poison Sumac has white berries and grows mainly in wet areas, differentiating it from other sumacs which have red berries.

Edible Uses: Many species, like the Staghorn and Smooth Sumac, have red berries that can be used to make a tangy, lemonade-like drink. The berries are soaked in cold water, mashed, strained, and sweetened to taste. Native Americans and early settlers often used the berries as a seasoning, and they can also be dried and ground into a spice.

Medicinal Uses: Different Native American tribes historically used sumac species for various medicinal purposes, including treating respiratory and digestive complaints, fevers, and wounds. The bark and roots were often used in traditional medicines for their astringent properties.

Other Uses: Sumac berries have been used as a natural dye, producing shades of red. The tannin-rich bark and leaves can be used for tanning leather.

Robinia pseudoacacia

Common Name: Black Locust, False Acacia

Family: Fabaceae

Description: The Black Locust, scientifically known as Robinia pseudoacacia, is a deciduous tree that prominently belongs to the Fabaceae family. This resilient tree can grow up to 30 meters in height and is characterized by its deeply furrowed bark and spiny shoots. During late spring, the tree showcases cascading clusters of fragrant, white, pea-like flowers that are not only a sight to behold but also magnetize bees, essential for its pollination. Given its hardy nature, it can tolerate a range of conditions and often becomes a natural boundary in many landscapes due to its rapid spread and growth.

Known Hazards: The bark and the leaves of the Black Locust are toxic when ingested, containing compounds known as robinetin and robitin, which can lead to symptoms like nausea, vomiting, and diarrhea. It is imperative to exercise caution, especially around children and pets.

Habitats: Black Locust thrives in well-drained soils and can often be found gracing pastures, edges of forests, and alongside roads. It's particularly adept at rejuvenating disturbed habitats and can often be one of the first trees to appear in cleared lands.

Range: Native to the southeastern United States, this tree has expanded its dominion, establishing itself across North America and even parts of Europe and Asia, often considered invasive in regions outside its native range.

Identification: Identifying the Black Locust is made easier by observing its compound leaves consisting of 7-19 leaflets. These are dark green on top and paler beneath. Its distinct flowers hang in pendulous racemes, resembling a cascade of white pearls. The tree's deeply ridged and dark bark provides another clue. Once the flowering is over, the tree produces smooth, flat pods containing 4-8 seeds. The pods, initially green, turn brown upon maturing.

Edible Uses: While caution is advised due to the tree's toxic parts, the flower blossoms of the Black Locust can be safely consumed. They make for delightful fritters when dipped in batter and fried. The flowers can also be infused to make aromatic syrups or floral jams.

Medicinal Uses: Historically, Black Locust's inner bark was brewed into a tea to treat ailments such as whooping cough and asthma. Its anti-spasmodic properties were revered in traditional medicine.

Externally, a poultice made from the bark provided relief from skin ailments. However, it's crucial to approach its medicinal use with caution given its toxic nature.

Rubus spp.

Common Name: Blackberries, Raspberries, Dewberries

Family: Rosaceae

Description: The Rubus genus encompasses a variety of deciduous shrubs, commonly known for their delicious berries. These plants are characterized by their thorny stems and dark green leaves. Depending on the species, they can grow between 1 to 3 meters in height. The berries range from red, black, or purple when ripe, attracting a variety of wildlife.

Known Hazards: The plant's thorny stems can cause skin irritation. Consuming unripe berries or large quantities of the leaves may cause gastrointestinal distress.

Habitats: These plants are highly adaptable and grow well in a range of soil types but prefer well-drained, fertile soils. They are commonly found in woodlands, fields, and along roadsides.

Range: The Rubus genus has a broad distribution, native to various regions worldwide including North America, Europe, and Asia.

Identification: The leaves are usually compound, with three to five leaflets that have serrated edges. Flowers, typically white or pink, appear in clusters and give way to the distinctive berries. Each berry is a cluster of tiny, individual drupelets surrounding a core.

Edible Uses: The berries are a popular fruit, consumed fresh, or used in jams, jellies, and baked goods. Young shoots and leaves are also edible when cooked.

Medicinal Uses: Leaves from the Rubus genus, especially raspberry leaves, have been used in herbal teas to aid in digestion and are believed to have various health benefits including anti-inflammatory properties.

Other Uses: The strong, flexible stems have been traditionally used for weaving baskets. The berries can also be used as natural dyes.

Rumex acetosella

Common Name: Sheep's Sorrel, Red Sorrel, Sour Weed
Family: Polygonaceae
Description: Rumex acetosella, commonly known as Sheep's Sorrel, is a perennial herb that belongs to the buckwheat family. It's often characterized by its arrow-shaped leaves and tall, reddish-green flowering stems. Due to its sour taste, it has historically been used as a flavoring in dishes and is considered by many to be a weed, especially in pastures where it competes with grass.

Known Hazards: Oxalic acid is found in sheep's sorrel, especially in significant quantities in the leaves. While not directly toxic in small amounts, excessive consumption can inhibit the body's absorption of calcium and can be harmful to individuals with kidney disorders, rheumatism, or hyperacidity. Furthermore, its prolonged use or ingestion in large amounts can lead to poisoning.

Habitats: Sheep's Sorrel typically thrives in acidic, sandy soils. You'll often find it in fields, meadows, and pastures, as well as along roadsides and waste places. It's quite resilient and can establish itself in a range of environments, including those disturbed by human activity.

Range: This hardy plant has a vast distribution and can be found in various parts of the world, including Europe, Asia, and North America.

Identification: Sheep's Sorrel is identified by its distinctive arrow-shaped leaves that often have a pair of pointed lobes at their base. As the seasons progress, slender, upright stems emerge, producing tiny red flowers that evolve into small, triangular fruits. The leaves are where its sour taste is most pronounced, a result of the oxalic acid content.

Edible Uses: The leaves of Sheep's Sorrel are edible and have a tangy, lemon-like flavor. They can be consumed raw in salads, soups, or used as a garnish. In the past, it was also used to curdle milk and produce a type of cheese. However, due to its high oxalic acid content, consumption should be in moderation.

Medicinal Uses: Traditionally, Sheep's Sorrel has been employed for various medicinal purposes. Its leaves, when crushed and applied topically, have been used to alleviate inflammation and dry skin. A tea made from the leaves was once believed to reduce fever and aid in digestion. Some herbalists claim its roots can be beneficial as a diuretic, while others have used it as an agent to induce vomiting. However, given its oxalic acid content, caution is always advised.

Sagittaria spp.

Common Name: Arrowhead, Duck Potato, Wapato
Family: Alismataceae
Description: Sagittaria is a genus of aquatic plants often found in shallow wetlands and the edges of ponds and streams. The name "Arrowhead" is derived from the distinctive arrow-shaped leaves. The plants can vary in size, from small species that are just a few inches tall to larger ones reaching several feet in height. They typically produce white, three-petaled flowers.

Known Hazards: While many species within the Sagittaria genus are edible, it's crucial to correctly identify the specific species before consumption. Some species may contain calcium oxalate crystals, which can cause irritation to the skin and mucous membranes.

Habitats: Sagittaria species are usually found in aquatic or semi-aquatic environments, including ponds, marshes, slow streams, and wet ditches. They prefer shallow water but can tolerate slightly deeper conditions, depending on the species.

Range: These plants are primarily native to the Americas, but some species can be found in parts of Europe, Asia, and Africa.

Identification: The most distinctive feature of the Sagittaria is its arrow-shaped leaves, which rise directly from the base of the plant. These leaves can either float on the water's surface or stand erect above the waterline. The flowers are typically white, with three petals, and form in whorls of three on a single stalk that emerges above the foliage. The tubers or "duck potatoes" are buried in the mud and can vary in size, often resembling small potatoes. The shape and size of the leaves, as well as the specific habitat conditions, can help in identifying the exact species of Sagittaria.

Edible Uses: The tubers, commonly referred to as "duck potatoes", are the most widely consumed part of the plant. They can be eaten raw, though they're more commonly boiled, roasted, or fried. They have a starchy texture and a taste reminiscent of potatoes or chestnuts. Some species also have edible shoots and young leaves, which can be consumed after cooking.

Medicinal Uses: Historically, certain indigenous communities have used parts of Sagittaria plants for medicinal purposes, such as treating indigestion and wounds. However, its contemporary medicinal applications are not well-documented.

Sambucus canadensis

Common Name: American Elderberry

Family: Adoxaceae

Description: Sambucus canadensis, or American Elderberry, is a deciduous shrub that can grow up to 4 meters in height. It blooms clusters of small, white flowers from late spring to early summer, which later mature into dark purple-black berries by late summer to early autumn. The shrub is a popular choice for both ornamental and functional plantings.

Known Hazards: Although the ripe berries and flowers are edible, all other parts of the plant, including the leaves, stems, and unripe berries, contain toxic compounds and should be avoided.

Habitats: The American Elderberry is versatile and can adapt to various environments but prefers moist, well-drained soils. It's commonly found in wetlands, along rivers, and in open woodlands.

Range: Native to North America, it is widespread across the United States and parts of Canada.

Identification: This shrub boasts compound leaves divided into 5–11 leaflets, each with sharply serrated edges. The flowers appear in large, flat-topped clusters and are a cream-white color. These give way to drooping clusters of round, dark purple to almost black berries.

Edible Uses: The ripe berries are a rich source of nutrients and are often used in jams, jellies, and syrups. The flowers are also edible and can be used to make teas or flavored liqueurs.

Medicinal Uses: Traditionally, the flowers and berries have been used for their anti-inflammatory, diuretic, and immune-boosting properties. They are also said to help alleviate symptoms of colds and flu.

Other Uses: It can be used for natural dyeing purposes.

Smilax herbacea

Common Name: Carrion Flower, Smooth Carrion Flower, Smooth Herbaceous Greenbrier

Family: Smilacaceae

Description: Smilax herbacea is a perennial, climbing vine that belongs to the Smilacaceae family. Native to eastern North America, it can grow up to 4 meters tall, supported by tendrils that help it attach to nearby vegetation. The plant features alternate, broad, and heart-shaped leaves. Notably, it emits an unpleasant odor, especially when its greenish-yellow flowers are in bloom, usually from late spring to early summer. The flowers then give way to clusters of bluish-black berries by late summer.

Known Hazards: While not toxic, the plant's unpleasant smell can be off-putting, and it's advisable to handle it carefully to avoid the odor sticking to your hands.

Habitat: Smilax herbacea thrives in a variety of settings including forests, woodlands, and thickets. It is highly adaptable to different soil conditions but prefers moist, well-drained soils.

Range: This vine is primarily found in the eastern United States and parts of southeastern Canada, from Florida to southern Ontario and as far west as Texas and Nebraska.

Identification: The distinguishing features of Smilax herbacea are its heart-shaped leaves, which are broad and usually have smooth edges. The tendrils emerging from the leaf axils aid in climbing. Its greenish-yellow flowers, arranged in umbels, are easily recognized by their strong, foul odor. By late summer, these flowers transition into clusters of dark bluish-black berries, which can be another helpful identification characteristic. In identifying Smilax herbacea, pay attention to its heart-shaped leaves and strong, unpleasant odor, particularly when the greenish-yellow flowers are in bloom. By late summer, the appearance of dark bluish-black berries can also serve as an identifying feature. Always remember to handle the plant carefully to avoid its persistent odor.

Edible Uses: The young shoots and leaves of Smilax herbacea can be consumed either raw or cooked, often used in salads or as a green vegetable. The roots can be harvested to make a sarsaparilla-type beverage, and the fruit, while not particularly palatable, is also edible.

Medicinal Uses: Although not as well-known for its medicinal properties, some traditional uses include the root for treating skin conditions and as a general tonic. However, its efficacy in a medicinal context has not been extensively studied.

Other Uses: Its aromatic roots may serve as a fragrance component in traditional practices.

Stellaria media

Common Name: Common Chickweed

Family: Caryophyllaceae

Description: Stellaria media, or Common Chickweed, is an annual or perennial herbaceous plant that is native to Europe but has naturalized across the globe. It grows in clusters, reaching heights of 15 to 45 cm and sports small, white, star-shaped flowers that bloom mainly from late winter to spring. The plant is often considered a weed but is also prized for its culinary and medicinal uses.

Known Hazards: While generally safe for consumption, it's essential to note that Chickweed may cause dermatitis in some individuals when applied topically.

Habitats: Chickweed thrives in a variety of environments, from gardens and lawns to fields and forests. It prefers moist, nitrogen-rich soils and often grows in shaded areas.

Range: Originally from Europe, it has now spread to North America, Asia, and other continents, adapting well to varying climates.

Identification: Stellaria media is distinguished by its small, oval leaves that grow opposite each other on slender, trailing stems. Its most defining feature is the small, white, star-shaped flowers, each with five deeply-notched petals, which can make them appear as if they have ten. The plant also has a line of fine hairs running down one side of the stem, switching sides at each pair of opposite leaves.

Edible Uses: Chickweed leaves, stems, and flowers are all edible. They can be consumed raw in salads or cooked like spinach. It has a mild, grassy taste and is rich in nutrients like vitamins and minerals.

Medicinal Uses: Traditionally, Chickweed has been used for its anti-inflammatory, diuretic, and expectorant properties. It has been applied topically for skin conditions like rashes and eczema and consumed as a tea for respiratory ailments.

Other Uses: Some also use it as a green manure to enrich the soil, given its nitrogen-loving nature.

Taraxacum officinale

Common Name: Dandelion

Family: Asteraceae

Description: Taraxacum officinale, commonly known as the dandelion, is a perennial herbaceous plant with a global distribution. It forms a basal rosette of leaves and produces bright yellow flower heads that mature into iconic, wind-dispersed seed heads often referred to as "dandelion clocks." The plant can grow up to 45 cm in height and is one of the most recognizable wild plants due to its distinct flowers and fluffy seed heads.

Known Hazards: While mostly safe for consumption, some people may experience allergic reactions. The plant also has a diuretic effect, so caution is advised for those with kidney issues.

Habitats: Dandelions are incredibly adaptable, thriving in a wide range of environments, from meadows and grasslands to urban areas. They prefer full sun but can tolerate partial shade.

Range: Originally from Eurasia, it has now naturalized in North America, South America, and other parts of the world.

Identification: Dandelions are identified by their serrated, lanceolate leaves that form a basal rosette. The bright yellow flower heads sit atop hollow, unbranched stems filled with milky latex. As the flowers mature, they transform into spherical seed heads comprised of numerous parachute-like seeds designed for wind dispersal.

Edible Uses: Nearly all parts of the dandelion are edible. The leaves can be used in salads or cooked like spinach, the flowers can be used to make syrups or fritters, and the roots can be roasted to make a coffee substitute.

Medicinal Uses: The dandelion has been used in traditional medicine for its diuretic, anti-inflammatory, and liver detoxifying properties. Its leaves and roots are often consumed as teas, tinctures, or capsules.

Other Uses: The latex from the dandelion stem has been explored as a natural rubber source. The plant is also used in some cosmetics and skincare products due to its high antioxidant content.

68

Tilia americana

Common Name: American Basswood, Carolina Basswood, Basswood, American Linden

Family: Tiliaceae

Description: The American Basswood, also known as the Carolina Basswood or American Linden, is a deciduous tree that's distinct within the Tiliaceae family. This tree, known for its rapid growth, can reach up to 25 meters in height with a spread of around 12 meters. During July, it blooms with fragrant flowers which give way to seeds by October. Both male and female organs exist on the same plant, making it hermaphrodite, and it's a beacon for bees that play a pivotal role in its pollination. Wildlife is often attracted to this tree, making it a hub of activity.

Known Hazards: It's important to proceed with caution when consuming the tea made from its flowers. Frequent consumption can cause heart damage. Always use the fresh flowers to avoid potential narcotic properties that might develop as they age.

Habitats: The Basswood thrives in rich, often moist soils, predominantly in woods and bottomlands. Often, it forms pure stands in these habitats.

Range: Its natural habitat stretches across Central and Eastern North America. This includes regions from New Brunswick to Florida and extends westwards to Texas and Manitoba.

Identification: The tree boasts heart-shaped leaves that have an asymmetrical base, ranging between 5-15 cm in length, with finely serrated edges. These leaves possess a bright green hue on their upper surface and a lighter, sometimes almost silvery, underside. During its flowering season in July, the Basswood comes alive with clusters of small, creamy-yellow flowers. These drooping clusters hang from a unique, elongated, leaf-like bract. As the seasons change, these flowers give way to small, round, and hard fruit, often referred to as 'nutlets.' These are about the size of peas and dangle beneath the same leafy bracts. The bark of a young Basswood tree remains smooth and light gray, but as it ages, it becomes ridged and furrowed. To further your identification confidence, crush a leaf; you'll be met with a distinctly mellow, somewhat floral scent which is a characteristic of the Tilia Americana.

Edible Uses: Venturing into its culinary offerings, young leaves from the Basswood can be consumed both raw and cooked, making them a delightful addition to salads. The sap, found adjacent to the bark, doubles as a refreshing drink and, when concentrated, a sweetener in the form of syrup. Its fragrant flowers are not only edible but also serve as a tea substitute. A unique treat is the chocolate substitute, crafted from a blend of ground fruits and flowers of the tree.

Medicinal Uses: An inner bark tea is beneficial for soothing burns, softening the skin, and providing relief for respiratory and digestive complaints linked to anxiety. The bark possesses diuretic properties, promoting urination. This tree's blooms, whether fresh or dried, have properties that are antispasmodic, diaphoretic, and sedative, making them remedies for ailments like hypertension, migraines, and arterial issues. The leaves, on the other hand, have been employed as eyewashes or poultices for burns and fractures. Furthermore, a concoction derived from the roots is known to be effective against internal hemorrhages and as a vermifuge against worms.

Other Uses: Beyond the realm of consumption and medicinal use, the inner bark yields a durable fiber which, once processed, can be transformed into threads, yarns, or cordages. This is utilized in creating an array of items like nets, twine, and mats.

Trifolium spp.

Common Name: Clover

Family: Fabaceae

Description: Trifolium, commonly known as clover, is a genus within the Fabaceae family. It consists of herbaceous perennial or annual plants that are often low-growing and found in a variety of habitats. Depending on the species, the height can vary, but most are characterized by their trifoliate leaves and spherical flower heads that range in color from white to purple.

Known Hazards: Some species contain cyanogenic glycosides and can be toxic if consumed in large quantities. Always properly identify the species before consumption.

Habitats: Clovers thrive in a range of environments, including meadows, grasslands, and open woodlands, preferring well-drained soil.

Range: The Trifolium genus has a worldwide distribution but is most common in temperate regions of the Northern Hemisphere.

Identification: Clovers are distinguished by their trifoliate leaves, usually composed of three ovoid or elliptical leaflets. The flower heads are quite distinctive, usually spherical and made up of numerous tiny florets. Depending on the species, these can be white, pink, red, or purple. The leaves may also feature a lighter or darker 'V' or crescent-shaped marking.

Edible Uses: Clovers are edible and can be used in salads, soups, and teas. The young leaves are best picked before the plant flowers, as this is when they are most tender.

Medicinal Uses: Clover is rich in nutrients and has been traditionally used for its blood-cleansing properties. Some species are known to have antispasmodic, expectorant, and anti-inflammatory qualities.

Typha angustifolia

Common Name: Narrowleaf Cattail, Lesser Bulrush

Family: Typhaceae

Description: Typha angustifolia, commonly known as the Narrowleaf Cattail, is a perennial herbaceous plant that belongs to the Typhaceae family. It typically reaches heights between 1.5 to 3 meters. The plant has long, slender, gray-green leaves and a tall, rigid stem topped with a brown, cigar-shaped flowering spike. This spike, which is a distinguishing feature of cattails, consists of thousands of tiny flowers.

Habitats: Typha angustifolia thrives in wetlands, marshes, and the edges of ponds and lakes. They are commonly found in shallow water, often forming dense colonies.

Range: This cattail species is native to North America and Europe, but its adaptability has led it to spread to various other parts of the world.

Identification: To identify Typha angustifolia, look for its slender leaves and the characteristic brown, cigar-shaped flowering spike. The plant typically has a gap between the male and female parts of its flowering spike, which can help differentiate it from other closely related cattail species.

Edible Uses: Various parts of the Narrowleaf Cattail are edible. The young shoots can be eaten raw or cooked, tasting somewhat like cucumber or zucchini. The roots are starchy and can be consumed after thorough cooking; they are sometimes processed into flour. The pollen from the flower spike can also be harvested and used as a flour substitute or additive.

Medicinal Uses: Historically, the cattail plant has been used for its antiseptic properties. The gel-like substance between the young leaves was applied to wounds, cuts, and burns. Additionally, certain preparations from the plant were used to treat ailments like kidney stones and dysentery. It's essential to consult a healthcare professional before using any plant for medicinal purposes.

Other Uses: Beyond edibility and potential medicinal uses, Typha angustifolia has been employed in various practical applications. The fluffy seeds have been used as insulation and stuffing, while the robust leaves and stems were utilized for making mats, baskets, and even shelter in some indigenous cultures.

Urtica dioica

Common Name: Stinging Nettle

Family: Urticaceae

Description: Urtica dioica, widely recognized as Stinging Nettle, is a perennial herbaceous plant that can grow up to 1 to 2 meters tall. Its square stems bear oppositely arranged leaves, with coarsely toothed margins. The plant's most distinct feature is the presence of minute, hair-like structures filled with irritating compounds on the stems and the undersides of the leaves. When touched, these hairs break off and can release the compounds, leading to a stinging sensation on the skin.

Known Hazards: The hairs or "spines" of the stinging nettle release formic acid, histamine, and other chemicals that can cause a burning sensation upon contact with skin. The sting can lead to redness, swelling, and itchiness. It's essential to handle the plant with gloves or other protection. However, once cooked or dried, the stinging properties disappear.

Habitats: Stinging Nettles are versatile in terms of habitat. They flourish in rich, moist soils, often in disturbed areas, alongside roads, trails, or at the edges of woods. They are also frequently found near streams or in open meadows.

Range: This plant is native to Europe, Asia, northern Africa, and North America. Due to its wide adaptability, it can be found in many parts of the world, often naturalized outside its native range.

Identification: Identifying the Stinging Nettle is relatively straightforward due to its unique characteristics. The leaves are lance-shaped, with a pointed tip and serrated edges. The aforementioned stinging hairs, primarily on the underside of the leaves and stem, are a notable feature. During its flowering season, the plant exhibits small, inconspicuous greenish or brownish flowers, which hang in slender, string-like clusters from the leaf axils.

Edible Uses: Despite its stinging property, the Stinging Nettle is remarkably nutritious. Young leaves, when cooked, serve as a spinach substitute, boasting a rich content of vitamins A and C, iron, potassium, manganese, and calcium. The leaves can be steamed, sautéed, or added to soups. Seeds and roots are also occasionally used in culinary applications.

Medicinal Uses: Urtica dioica has been employed in traditional medicine for centuries. It's been utilized as a diuretic and a remedy for arthritis and muscle pain. The plant has anti-inflammatory properties and is sometimes taken to alleviate allergy symptoms. Recent studies suggest potential benefits for prostate health, though more research is required in this area. Externally, nettle has been used to treat skin conditions, and the sting itself, surprisingly, has been used in "urtication" therapy to alleviate joint pain.

Other Uses: Beyond food and medicine, Stinging Nettle fibers have historically been used to create cloth, similar in texture to linen. Its durable threads have been utilized for making cordage. Nettles are also used as a natural dye, yielding a green color from the leaves and a yellow from the roots.

Vaccinium macrocarpon

Common Name: American Cranberry, Large Cranberry

Family: Ericaceae

Description: The American Cranberry, or Vaccinium macrocarpon, is a low-growing, trailing, woody perennial shrub, a distinguished member of the Ericaceae family. This evergreen shrub typically ranges in height from 5-20 cm and spreads horizontally, sometimes up to 2 meters. During late spring to early summer, its branches produce small, pinkish-white flowers that eventually yield the well-known red fruit by late summer to early autumn.

Known Hazards: Generally considered safe for consumption, the American Cranberry poses minimal risk. However, excessive consumption of cranberry juice may lead to gastrointestinal upset. It is always advised to consult healthcare providers when consuming cranberry products alongside medications, as interactions may occur.

Habitats: The American Cranberry thrives in acidic, peat-rich, sandy soils commonly found in bogs, swamps, and other wetlands. These conditions are particularly crucial for the plant's survival and fruit production.

Range: Native to northeastern North America, it spans from the eastern United States to eastern Canada. It has also been cultivated in other parts of the world, including Europe.

Identification: This species is recognizable for its small, elliptic leaves that are glossy on the upper surface and matte underneath. The flowers, usually pale pink or white, are bell-shaped and hang in loose clusters. By late summer or early fall, these flowers give way to the characteristic round, red cranberries, which are approximately 1-2 cm in diameter.

Edible Uses: The fruit of Vaccinium macrocarpon is highly valued for its tart flavor and is often processed into juices, jellies, and sauces. They are also dried and consumed as snacks or included in various baked goods.

Medicinal Uses: The cranberries from this plant have been studied for their potential in preventing urinary tract infections due to the presence of proanthocyanidins, which inhibit bacterial adhesion to the urinary tract. They also contain vitamin C and other antioxidants and have been researched for their cardiovascular benefits, although more studies are needed to establish these claims conclusively.

Viburnum lentago

Common Name: Nannyberry, Sheepberry, Sweet Viburnum

Family: Adoxaceae

Description: The Nannyberry, also commonly referred to as Sheepberry or Sweet Viburnum, is a native North American shrub or tree that can reach heights of up to 6-9 meters. The plant is distinguished by its opposite, lance-shaped leaves, fragrant white flowers that bloom in spring, and dark blue-black fruit that matures in early autumn. The fruit is edible and has a sweet and pleasant taste. It's noteworthy for its adaptability, being able to flourish in a range of soils and conditions.

Known Hazards: There are no significant known hazards associated with this plant when consumed in moderation. However, like many plants, excessive consumption may lead to stomach upset.

Habitats: Nannyberry is frequently found in moist sites, including stream banks, swamps, open woods, and thickets. They prefer well-drained soils but can adapt to a variety of soil types.

Range: This plant is native to North America, with its range extending from southeastern Canada, throughout the eastern and central United States, and into the central Great Plains.

Identification: Identifying the Nannyberry involves looking for its characteristic features. The leaves are opposite, simple, and lanceolate, with finely toothed margins. In spring, the plant blooms with white, fragrant flower clusters that are typically 10-15 cm across. By early autumn, these give way to blue-black, oval-shaped drupes that are around 1 cm long. The bark of Nannyberry is grayish-brown and becomes more furrowed and rough with age. In the fall, the foliage can take on impressive red and purple hues, adding to its ornamental value.

Edible Uses: The berries of the Nannyberry are edible, with a sweet, raisin-like taste. They can be consumed fresh or can be used to make jellies, jams, or syrups. The large seed within, however, is inedible.

Medicinal Uses: While Viburnum lentago isn't prominently known for its medicinal uses, some Native American tribes historically used parts of the plant for medicinal purposes, including treating cramps and menstrual disorders.

Viburnum trilobum

Common Name: American Cranberrybush, High Bush Cranberry, Cranberry Viburnum, Crampbark

Family: Adoxaceae

Description: Viburnum trilobum, more recently classified as Viburnum edule, is a deciduous shrub typically growing between 2 to 4 meters in height. The plant is distinguishable by its maple-like leaves, which are three-lobed and have a serrated margin. During spring, the shrub produces white flowers in flat-topped corymbs. By fall, it bears bright red berries that persist throughout winter.

Known Hazards: While the fruits are edible, they can be mildly toxic if consumed in large quantities, causing diarrhea or an upset stomach. It's important to consume them in moderation.

Habitats: It's commonly found in damp woods, swamps, and bogs, as well as along streambanks and shores. The plant prefers well-drained soils and can tolerate a variety of pH levels.

Range: Native to the northeastern and midwestern regions of North America, stretching from Newfoundland west to British Columbia and south to Washington and Oregon.

Identification: Look for a medium-sized shrub with maple-like leaves and clusters of white flowers. By autumn, these give way to bright red berries that remain on the shrub even after leaf fall.

Edible Uses: The berries are edible, both raw and cooked, though they might be bitter when raw. They can be made into jellies, sauces, or jams. It's common to mix them with other fruits, especially sweet ones, to offset the bitterness.

Medicinal Uses: Historically, the bark has been used as a muscle relaxant, hence the name "Crampbark." Indigenous peoples have used parts of the plant for various medicinal applications, such as easing menstrual cramps or treating kidney issues. As always, it's crucial to consult a professional before using plants for medicinal purposes.

Viola sororia

Common Name: Common Blue Violet, Woolly Blue Violet, Sister Violet

Family: Violaceae

Description: Viola sororia, often recognized as the Common Blue Violet or Woolly Blue Violet, is a low-growing, herbaceous perennial belonging to the Violaceae family. Native to eastern North America, this violet stands about 10-20 cm tall and has heart-shaped leaves that are frequently covered in fine hairs. The distinctive blue-purple flowers emerge from the late winter into spring. These flowers are hermaphroditic, possessing both male and female reproductive organs.

Known Hazards: While Viola sororia is largely considered safe for consumption, it's advisable to avoid the rhizome, which can be emetic. As always, accurate identification is crucial before foraging.

Habitats: This violet species is highly adaptable, often found in diverse conditions ranging from woodlands to lawns, and even wet meadows. It favors well-drained, loamy soils but is not particularly fussy about its living conditions.

Range: Viola sororia is commonly found in the eastern regions of the United States and extends into Canada. It has also been naturalized in certain parts of Europe.

Identification: The plant features heart-shaped, dark green leaves typically measuring 5-10 cm in width. These leaves often have a slightly serrated margin. The flowers range from deep violet to blue-purple, sometimes even white, and are usually 2-3 cm in diameter. They possess five rounded petals, with the bottom petal often featuring a white 'beard'.

Edible Uses: The leaves and flowers of Viola sororia are edible. The young leaves can be consumed raw in salads or cooked like spinach. The flowers, with their gentle, sweet flavor, make delightful garnishes for desserts and drinks or can be used in salads.

Medicinal Uses: In traditional medicine, the leaves are known for their mild diuretic properties and have been used to treat urinary tract issues. The plant is also thought to possess mild anti-inflammatory effects, although scientific backing for these claims is limited.

Vitis riparia

Common Name: Riverbank Grape, Wild Grape

Family: Vitaceae

Description: Vitis riparia, known as the riverbank grape, is a vigorous, deciduous vine native to North America. It's recognized for its adaptability to various soil types and its cold-hardiness, making it a crucial species for breeding cold-resistant grape varieties. The vine features deep green leaves, clusters of greenish flowers that bloom in late spring, and small, dark purple to black grapes that ripen in the fall.

Known Hazards: All parts of the plant, except the ripe fruit, contain substances that can be toxic if consumed in large quantities. The sap can cause skin irritation in some individuals.

Habitats: As its common name suggests, Vitis riparia typically thrives along riverbanks, stream edges, and in moist woodlands. It can also be found along roadsides and in clearings, often clambering over other vegetation or structures.

Range: This wild grape is native to North America and is widespread throughout the central and eastern United States and Canada.

Identification: Vitis riparia has heart-shaped to palmately lobed leaves that are serrated along the edges. The leaves are often shiny on the upper surface and paler, sometimes with a slight fuzz, beneath. In late spring, the plant produces inconspicuous greenish-yellow flowers arranged in clusters. By late summer to early fall, these give way to clusters of small, round grapes. The grapes are usually dark purple to black when ripe, although color can vary. The bark on older stems shreds and peels.

Edible Uses: The ripe grapes of Vitis riparia can be eaten fresh, though they are tart in flavor. They are often used to make jellies, jams, and wine. It's essential to ensure the grapes are ripe before consumption, as unripe grapes and other plant parts can be mildly toxic.

Medicinal Uses: Historically, Native American tribes have used the riverbank grape for various medicinal purposes. The roots were used to treat digestive issues, and the vine's sap was applied as a treatment for sore eyes. The leaves were occasionally used as poultices for sore breasts, wounds, and inflammations.

Zizania aquatica, Z. palustris

Common Name: Wild Rice, Annual Wild Rice (for Z. aquatica), Northern Wild Rice (for Z. palustris)

Family: Poaceae

Description: Belonging to the grass family, wild rice is not truly a rice but a distinct grain altogether. Both species grow in shallow water in slow-flowing streams, lakes, and ponds. Their tall, graceful stems rise several feet above the water, capped with elegant, drooping seed heads that sway with the breeze. Historically, wild rice has been a crucial staple for indigenous peoples of North America, both as a source of nutrition and for its cultural and spiritual significance.

Known Hazards: None known

Habitats: Both Z. aquatica and Z. palustris prefer shallow water habitats, such as lakes, ponds, and slow-moving streams. They thrive in fresh to brackish waters and require sunlit conditions.

Range: Wild rice is native to North America, especially prevalent in the Great Lakes region and the central United States. Z. palustris is more widespread in the northern regions, while Z. aquatica has a more southerly distribution.

Identification: Wild rice can be recognized by its tall, grass-like appearance growing out of water bodies. The seed heads, forming at the top of the plant, are loose, branching panicles bearing the long-grained seeds. When mature, these grains have a characteristic dark color. The two species can be differentiated primarily by their geography and minor differences in grain size and color.

Edible Uses: Wild rice grains are highly nutritious and can be boiled or steamed like conventional rice. They have a nutty flavor and chewy texture. Often, they are mixed with other grains or used in salads, soups, or casseroles. Besides the grain, young wild rice shoots can also be eaten, typically boiled.

Medicinal Uses: Traditionally, parts of the wild rice plant were used by indigenous peoples for medicinal purposes. For instance, a decoction of the stem was used as a wash for sore muscles. The grains were also believed to have restorative properties and were sometimes used as a dietary supplement for the sick.

SUBMIT A REVIEW

If you enjoyed this chapter, I would be grateful if you could support me by leaving a review of the book on Amazon. Your feedback is very valuable and inspires me!

It's very simple and only takes a few minutes:

1. Go to the "My Orders" page on Amazon and search for the book "Forager's Harvest 101".

2. Select "Write a product review".

3. Select a Star Rating.

4. Optionally, add text, photos, or videos and select Submit.

Chapter 4: Edible Wild Mushrooms

I n the wondrous tapestry of wild edibles, mushrooms occupy their own distinctive realm, an alchemy of earth, air, and a dash of magic. For millennia, humans have been captivated by these enigmatic organisms that spring forth in forests, fields, and even in the most unassuming corners of our lawns. Among them, edible fungi are especially cherished, offering both a culinary delicacy and myriad therapeutic benefits. However, mushrooms come with their own caveats—some are not merely toxic but fatally so. Thus, it is of paramount importance to possess a nuanced understanding of the multifaceted world of mushrooms, allowing us to appreciate their splendor while exercising caution.

The scenery of mushroom foraging can range from lush deciduous forests to the whispering pines of coniferous expanses, down to the quietude of meadows. The best time to hunt for most edible mushrooms is late summer through early fall. During these periods, you're likely to encounter varieties like the ever-popular morels, which favor deciduous terrains in the springtime, or the cepes—commonly known as porcini—reveling under pine trees as autumnal winds start to chill the air. Chanterelles, those golden gems of the forest floor, make their appearance in both summer and fall.

But what casts a shadow over this earthly marvel is the very real peril of poisonous mushrooms. From the infamous Death Cap to the Destroying Angel and the Fool's Mushroom, there are species out there that not only cause severe illness but can indeed be life-ending. While some toxic species might have benign doppelgangers, the stakes in mushroom foraging are too high for guesswork. If you are in doubt about the identification of a mushroom, the best policy is to forego sampling it until you can be sure. Cooking can mitigate the toxicity of certain types, but it's not a foolproof method for ensuring safety.

Black Trumpet (Craterellus cornucopioides)

Range: Spread widely across North America, especially in the eastern regions.

Habitat: These fungi have a predilection for moist, shaded woodlands, especially under hardwood trees like oaks. They often grow in clusters, hidden amidst the leaf litter, which can make them a challenging but rewarding find for the observant forager.

When: The best times to discover these elusive treats are during summer to early fall.

Identification: Their distinct trumpet or funnel shape, combined with the dark gray to black coloring, usually sets them apart. However, it's their lack of prominent gills and the smooth to veined underside of the cap that confirms their identity. Due to their dark hue, they often blend seamlessly with the forest floor, making them a treasure hunt for the keen-eyed forager.

Preparation: The Black Trumpet, despite its ominous nickname "Trumpet of Death", is a gastronomic delight. They're best cooked to release their deep, smoky, and fruity flavor - a quality that makes them highly prized in gourmet dishes. Sautéing them in butter or olive oil allows their flavor to shine. They're also excellent when dried and rehydrated, as the drying process intensifies their rich taste, making them a favored addition to sauces, soups, and risottos.

Chanterelle (Cantharellus cibarius)

Range: Widespread across the USA but more predominantly found in the Pacific Northwest, Northeast, and parts of the Southeast.

Habitat: This mushroom prefers woodland settings, often forming partnerships with hardwoods and conifers. It's commonly found in mossy forests, damp areas, or along pathways in dappled sunlight.

When: The chanterelle's season runs from late spring through to the fall, depending on the region.

Identification: The chanterelle's allure begins with its vibrant golden hue, reminiscent of the warm sun. Its cap, wavy and often curled at the edges, transitions smoothly to the stem. Unlike many mushrooms, Cantharellus cibarius boasts not gills but forked, cross-veined ridges underneath, which tend to be less defined and more vein-like than typical gills. The flesh is firm, and when torn, reveals a white inner layer. A distinctive feature aiding identification is its fruity aroma, often likened to apricots.

Preparation: The chanterelle's rich flavor and meaty texture are best showcased with simple preparations. Its water content is high, so when cooking, it's wise to first dry sauté, allowing its juices to release and then evaporate. This will intensify its flavor. Afterwards, add butter or oil and perhaps a hint of garlic or onion. The resulting sautéed mushrooms are an indulgence on their own or can be incorporated into sauces, pastas, or omelettes.

Chicken of the Woods (Laetiporus sulphureus)

Range: Widely distributed across North America, it's especially prevalent in the eastern states and the Pacific Northwest.

Habitat: Chicken of the Woods has an affinity for hardwoods, particularly oak, although it can sometimes be found on yew, cherry, and sweet chestnut trees. It's a saprophytic fungus, often growing on either standing dead trees or fallen logs, but occasionally on living trees as well.

When: Fruiting typically occurs from summer to early fall.

Identification: The bright orange-yellow shelves of Chicken of the Woods are quite an eye-catcher in the forest. With a top surface that's slightly rough and suede-like, it stands in contrast to the smooth, pore-covered underside. Young specimens are most desirable as they have a tender, succulent edge. Older mushrooms can be tough and fibrous. It's essential to be aware that while this mushroom is distinct, it should always be identified confidently to avoid confusion with other non-edible or toxic fungi.

Preparation: As its common name suggests, this mushroom has a taste and texture reminiscent of chicken meat. For the best culinary experience, use young, tender specimens. They can be sliced and sautéed in butter or oil, retaining their meaty texture. It's a fantastic meat substitute in dishes where chicken is used, such as in stir-fries, pies, or even grilled. Some individuals might be sensitive to this mushroom, so it's always recommended to try a small amount first.

Fairy Ring Mushroom (Marasmius oreades)

Range: This mushroom is found throughout North America, Europe, and other parts of the world.

Habitat: Marasmius oreades favors grassy areas, from lawns and meadows to grassy clearings in woods. The name "Fairy Ring" comes from the circular pattern in which these mushrooms often grow in grass, forming rings that expand outward over time.

When: Fruiting typically happens from late spring to early fall.

Identification: The tan to buff-colored caps and their preference for grassy areas, often forming characteristic rings, are telltale signs of Fairy Ring mushroom. The cap's transformation from convex in youth to flatter in age, often with a small umbo, is another distinguishing feature. One of its remarkable traits is its ability to revive after drying out; after a rain, previously shriveled mushrooms will rehydrate and appear fresh again. Always ensure proper identification, as there are other mushrooms that can grow in similar habitats.

Preparation: They can be sautéed in butter or oil, where their flavor shines. They also make a delightful addition to soups, stews, and risottos. Drying these mushrooms can intensify their flavors, making them a wonderful seasoning agent when ground into powder.

Giant Puffball (Calvatia gigantea)

Range: Scattered across the USA, but more commonly found in the eastern parts and the Midwest.

Habitat: This giant wonder tends to favor open spaces, gracing fields, meadows, and grassy clearings in woodlands. It particularly enjoys well-aerated soils and can often be found after rains in late summer.

When: Their grand display typically occurs from late summer to early autumn.

Identification: The sheer size of Gian Puffball makes it hard to overlook in open landscapes. Its spheroid shape, often compared to a soccer ball, is predominantly white when young. The smooth, sometimes slightly wrinkled surface takes on a yellowish or brownish hue as it ages. Inside, the firm white flesh stands in stark contrast to the powdery spore mass that develops over time. It's worth noting that this puffball should be consumed when its interior is uniformly white; the onset of spore development indicates it's past its prime for culinary use.

Preparation: The Giant Puffball is culinary simplicity at its finest. Start by peeling off its outer skin to reveal the pristine, white flesh. At this stage, it's important to ensure that the mushroom is entirely white inside without any hints of yellowing or greenish-brown spores. Slice it into thick steaks and pan-fry in butter or oil until golden brown on both sides. Its subtle, earthy flavor is a canvas, allowing it to seamlessly integrate into various dishes. From adding it to stir-fries, to dicing it into soups or stews, its velvety texture and mild taste make it a favorite.

Hedgehog Mushroom (Hydnum repandum)

Range: Spreading its charm across North America, this mushroom is common in temperate forests.

Habitat: The Hedgehog favors the company of both coniferous and hardwood trees, forming mycorrhizal relationships with them. Often, they're discovered on the forest floor, amidst the leaf litter and woody debris.

When: This enchanting mushroom makes its appearance from late summer through to fall.

Identification: The real allure of this mushroom lies beneath its cap. The soft spines, or teeth, drooping gracefully are its defining feature and an instant identifier. This toothed underside replaces the more commonly found gills or pores of other mushrooms. The cap itself can be a bit irregular, with an undulating edge, presenting in hues of pale orange or beige. The stem, robust and solid, matches the cap in color, adding to its consistent visual appeal.

Preparation: Beyond its captivating appearance, Hedgehog mushroom brings a mild, nutty flavor with a hint of sweetness to the table. Its texture, both firm and crunchy, is retained even after cooking, making it a delightful addition to various dishes. Once prepped, they can be sautéed in butter or olive oil, or incorporated into risottos, stews, and stir-fries.

Honey Mushroom (Armillaria mellea)

Range: Found throughout the USA, but particularly prevalent in temperate forested regions.

Habitat: This species has a penchant for wooded areas, making its home primarily on stumps, tree roots, or buried wood.

When: The most opportune time to find this mushroom is in the fall, though it can occasionally appear in late summer or early winter.

Identification: Honey mushroom captivates with its golden-brown cap, which might showcase radial fibers. As the mushroom ages, its cap transitions from a youthful convex shape to a more mature flattened form. The gills underneath provide a contrast in a delicate shade of white to cream and cling to the stem. The stem itself is an exhibit, with its distinct ring and often bulbous base. An intriguing feature of this mushroom is the black, root-like structures called rhizomorphs – which resemble boot laces – often found spreading under the bark or in the soil around the infected tree.

Preparation: Once properly cooked, their rich, nutty flavor makes them a delightful addition to various dishes. Sautéing them in butter with a hint of garlic releases their flavors beautifully. They can also grace risottos, stews, and pastas with their unique taste.

Lion's Mane (Genus Hericium)

Range: Found across North America, particularly in temperate hardwood forests.

Habitat: These saprophytic fungi exhibit a penchant for wounded or dead hardwood trees. Whether it's on fallen logs, decomposing stumps, or injured sections of living trees, they draw sustenance from the wood, playing their part in the forest's recycling process.

When: The prime time for spotting these shaggy beauties is from late summer to fall.

Identification: The unmistakable feature of Hericium species is their cascading icicle-like spines, which hang down from either a branched structure or a more solid, singular mass. These spines, typically ranging from 1 to 5 cm in length, are dense and give the mushroom its plush appearance. Their pristine white hue (which might age to a yellow or beige) is another distinguishing trait. The absence of a traditional cap or gills further differentiates them from many other fungi.

Preparation: The culinary charm of the Lion's Mane, lies in their delicate seafood-like texture, often likened to crab or lobster. Once cleaned, they're best sautéed in butter or olive oil, where their mild, sweet taste, reminiscent of the aforementioned seafood, truly comes to the forefront. Apart from simple sautéing, they can be incorporated into pastas, risottos, or even seafood dishes as a substitute.

Lobster Mushroom (Hypomyces lactifluorum)

Range: Found primarily in North America, especially in the Pacific Northwest, the Great Lakes, the Northeast, and parts of the Appalachian region.

Habitat: Lobster mushroom prefers hardwood forests, especially those that are home to the mushrooms it parasitizes, such as Russula and Lactarius species.

When: The Lobster Mushroom typically appears from mid-summer to early fall.

Identification: Standing out with its vivid red-orange hue, the Lobster Mushroom is quite distinguishable in the woodland floor. The parasitized mushroom undergoes significant alteration in structure and color. Its unique transformation is not just skin-deep; even the interior of the host adopts a vibrant hue. The Lobster Mushroom often feels dense and firm to the touch. The deformation and coloration make this fungal marvel easy to spot, but care should be taken to ensure it's free of decay or worm infestation.

Preparation: This mushroom is a forager's delight in the kitchen. Once cleaned, it can be diced and sautéed in butter or olive oil, which highlights its subtle seafood nuances. It's also an excellent addition to pasta dishes, risottos, or soups, where its distinct taste shines through. Because of its meaty consistency, some even use it as a substitute for certain seafood dishes.

Meadow Mushroom (Agaricus campestris)

Range: Across the USA, particularly in the temperate regions.

Habitat: Seek out open grasslands, pastures, meadows, and even lawns or parks that haven't been treated with pesticides.

When: Late summer to early fall, especially after rains.

Identification: Meadow mushroom is distinguished by its evolving cap - starting as a hemispherical shape, becoming convex, and eventually flattening with age. Its predominantly white hue may gain a hint of yellow over time. Beneath, the gills transition from a gentle pink in their youth to a dark, mature black. The white stem features a transient ring. Unlike some toxic look-alikes, this mushroom lacks a bulbous base. Additionally, when broken, it emits a subtle aroma, evoking aniseed or almonds.

Preparation: It can be enjoyed raw in salads for a crisp, earthy bite. When cooked, whether sautéed in butter with garlic, added to stir-fries, soups, or stews, its flavors intensify and deepen. Grilled, it offers a smoky charm and can even serve as a meat substitute in some dishes.

Morels (Morchella spp.)

Range: Morels can be found across North America and in many parts of Europe, Asia, and other continents.

Habitat: Morels have a fondness for woodland areas, especially those with ash, elm, tulip, and old apple trees. They can also be found in areas that have experienced recent fires or disturbances, earning them the moniker "fire morels" in some regions.

When: Springtime, typically after the first warm rain followed by warmer temperatures.

Identification: Morels are distinct in appearance with their mesh-like caps. However, caution is essential as the toxic false morel (Gyromitra spp.) bears a resemblance to true morels. The key difference is the interior: true morels are entirely hollow from the tip of the cap to the bottom of the stem. Additionally, the cap of a true morel is attached directly to the stem, not hanging freely from it as with some false morels.

Preparation: Morels are culinary treasures, hailed for their unique flavor and texture. After cleaning them (which often involves a soak to evict any critters), they can be sautéed in butter or oil, enhancing their nutty and earthy tones. They're a delightful addition to pastas, risottos, and other dishes.

Oyster Mushroom (Pleurotus ostreatus)

Range: Found throughout North America, Europe, Asia, and other parts of the world.

Habitat: Oyster mushrooms are wood lovers. They grow predominantly on dead hardwoods, although they've been known to colonize on some coniferous trees as well. They're frequently found on fallen logs or standing dead trees.

When: Typically in the cooler months of both spring and fall, but they can be found year-round in some climates.

Identification: Recognized by their distinct fan-shaped caps, which often grow in shelf-like clusters on wood. The lack of a prominent stem and the gills' decurrent nature (running down the cap's underside and onto the stem) is characteristic. One should always be cautious, as there are look-alikes like the poisonous Omphalotus nidiformis which glows in the dark.

Preparation: Oyster mushroom is highly esteemed in many cuisines for its delicate texture and subtle flavor. After cleaning them, they can be sautéed, grilled, or stir-fried. Their mild flavor lends itself well to a variety of dishes, from risottos to soups, or even served on toast. While they can be a centerpiece of a dish, they also complement other ingredients beautifully. They're tender, so they don't require long cooking times.

Porcino (Boletus edulis)

Range: Widespread across the USA, it's especially abundant in the Pacific Northwest and in the Northeastern states.

Habitat: Preferring the company of conifers and broadleaf trees, this mushroom is often found in forests, establishing a symbiotic relationship with living trees.

When: The mushroom is a herald of late summer to early fall, but depending on the region, it might make appearances from spring to late autumn.

Identification: The majesty of Porcino is evident from its broad, often large cap that wears hues ranging from rich browns to subtle tans. This color palette may sometimes be enriched with a tinge of red. Unlike many mushrooms, gills are absent. Instead, a spongy layer of tubes presents itself under the cap, transitioning from white in young specimens to a greenish hue in mature ones. The stem is a spectacle, robust and thick, with a distinctive white netted pattern gracing its upper section. A critical identifier is its solid flesh, which remains white and unchanging when sliced.

Preparation: Start by brushing off any debris, paying careful attention to the spongy undercap. Their meaty texture and earthy flavor are a standout in risottos, stews, and grilled preparations. A sauté in butter or olive oil, with a touch of herbs, transforms it into a gourmet delight. Drying is another popular preparation method, intensifying its flavors and ensuring it can be enjoyed throughout the year.

Shaggy Mane (Coprinus comatus)

Range: Distributed across North America, especially in temperate zones.

Habitat: Favored terrains include grassy areas, meadows, gardens, and roadsides. It's also common to find them bursting forth in disturbed soils, like those of newly seeded lawns or in woodchip mulches.

When: This ephemeral beauty is best sought from spring to fall, with its appearance often following rain.

Identification: The Shaggy Mane is distinct in its appearance, especially in its younger days, presenting a tall, white, cylindrical cap festooned with shaggy scales. As time progresses, the cap starts to unroll and eventually self-digests, leading to its inky namesake. The transformation of its gills, from white to pink and finally to an inky black, is a visual journey. The tall stem, with its transient ring, completes the look. A tip for foragers: young specimens, prior to the inky stage, are the most sought after.

Preparation: Shaggy Mane is best consumed soon after foraging, ideally within a few hours. When sautéed in butter or olive oil, the mushroom reveals a delicate flavor, often described as tender and slightly sweet. They can be a delightful addition to stir-fries, omelets, and even soups. However, it's worth noting, one should avoid alcohol when consuming this mushroom, as it can lead to adverse reactions in some individuals.

Wood Blewit (Clitocybe nuda)

Range: Widespread in North America, especially in the northern and western regions.

Habitat: This mushroom has an affinity for decomposing organic matter, making it a frequent visitor to woodlands, gardens, and leaf litter. While it doesn't grow directly on wood, it thrives in environments rich in decomposed wood or other organic materials.

When: The prime foraging period for Wood Blewit extends from late summer through to late autumn.

Identification: The Wood Blewit is easily recognizable for its lilac to purplish hues, though caution is needed as this color fades with age. The cap, while beginning as a convex form, broadens and flattens in mature specimens, showing off its unique color range. Its gills, moderately spaced, echo the lilac shades before darkening with time. The stem remains consistent in form, taking on the same color palette as the rest of the mushroom. A distinguishing trait is its slightly fragrant odor, which some describe as perfumed, and others liken to frozen orange juice.

Preparation: When it comes to the culinary stage, the Wood Blewit shines with versatility. Once cooked, its flavor profile, earthy and rich, lends itself well to various dishes. Sauteing in butter or olive oil draws out its best flavors, making it a delectable accompaniment to pastas, risottos, or as a side. Due to its robust nature, it also holds up well in stews and casseroles.

☆ ☆ ☆ ☆ ☆

SUBMIT A REVIEW

If you enjoyed this chapter, I would be grateful if you could support me by leaving a review of the book on Amazon. Your feedback is very valuable and inspires me!

It's very simple and only takes a few minutes:

1. Go to the "My Orders" page on Amazon and search for the book "Forager's Harvest 101".

2. Select "Write a product review".

3. Select a Star Rating.

4. Optionally, add text, photos, or videos and select Submit.

Chapter 5: Edible Wild Seaweeds

Venturing into the vast realms of wild edible seaweeds not only introduces one to unique flavors but also unravels their abundant nutritional virtues. As we delve into the art of gathering these marine greens, it's essential to maintain a vigilant approach, focusing on both our safety and the preservation of these delicate ecosystems. Ensuring personal safety while seaweed foraging is paramount. Familiarizing oneself with local regulations on seaweed harvest is a good starting point, as some regions might have specific guidelines in place to protect the environment and promote sustainability. Donning suitable attire is equally significant. Waterproof shoes, gloves, and protective outerwear can be one's best allies against unforeseen slips on unpredictable terrains and the occasional skin irritants that these coastal stretches might harbor.

Navigating rocky coastlines demands heightened caution. The rhythm of the tides, the unpredictable surge of waves, or the concealed sharp edges of rocks require continuous attention. Even the inhabitants of these marine landscapes, from the minuscule aquatic creatures to the more visible ones, can pose challenges if not approached with care. Lastly, the purity of the harvesting site is of utmost importance. The ideal locales for gathering seaweeds are those untouched by industrial imprints or the shadow of agricultural excesses. It's wise to distance oneself from regions in proximity to sewage outlets or industrial establishments, ensuring that the seaweeds' natural goodness remains uncontaminated.

While the oceanic bounty might seem vast and limitless, the act of gathering requires not just knowledge but also responsibility. It's paramount to approach this endeavor with an informed mind. Proper identification of seaweeds is essential. Missteps in this area could lead one to consume species that are either inedible or, in worse cases, toxic. Knowledge is the first layer of protection; always be certain about the seaweed species you're collecting.

Sustainable seaweed harvesting isn't just a recommendation, but a mandate for any conscientious forager. The marine ecosystem is delicate and requires thoughtful interaction. Always take only what you'll use, avoiding the pitfall of overharvesting which might destabilize the natural balance and potentially harm local marine biodiversity. It's also wise to diversify your harvesting locations. This approach not only ensures that specific areas aren't overharvested but also allows each region to naturally replenish its resources. When harvesting, it's also critical to be gentle: instead of uprooting the entire seaweed plant, selectively trim mature portions, ensuring the base remains intact. This practice encourages natural regrowth, keeping the cycle of life uninterrupted. Throughout the process, be ever vigilant to minimize disruption to other marine life and their habitats.

When it comes to the collection of seaweed samples, this can be both an educational endeavor and a testament to one's foraging journey. To ensure the integrity of your samples, utilize clean containers, clearly marking each with relevant details like date, location, and species name. Diversify your sampling from different locations and depths, as this can reveal variations in flavor, texture, and appearance. However, always keep different species separate to prevent any cross-contamination, preserving the intrinsic qualities of each seaweed.

After successfully collecting your seaweeds, the next step is the drying process. Initially, rinse the harvested seaweeds thoroughly in freshwater to remove any sand, salt, and small marine creatures that might be clinging on. With that done, separate the different types of seaweeds you've gathered and cut them into smaller, more manageable pieces if necessary. For air-drying, lay the seaweeds flat on a clean, dry surface situated in a well-ventilated area. If hanging them is more convenient, that works as well. It's important to note that indirect sunlight is best for maintaining their nutritional content. If you're looking for a quicker drying method, the oven serves as a good alternative. Set it to the lowest temperature, spread your seaweeds on a baking sheet, and leave the oven door slightly ajar to facilitate better air circulation. Once the seaweeds are fully dried, they should be stored in airtight containers and kept away from direct sunlight and moisture to preserve their quality.

Nori (Pyropia spp.)

Family: Bangiaceae

Description: Nori is a treasured seaweed that has been a central part of Asian cuisines for centuries, most notably in Japan. The deep green, almost black sheets of this marine plant have wrapped countless sushi rolls and rice balls, lending them a distinct umami flavor and a host of nutritional benefits. Nori's rise in popularity around the world can be attributed not only to the global love for sushi but also to its rich nutrient profile, which includes vital vitamins, minerals, and protein. Its cultivation and processing have become an art, reflecting the deep respect and appreciation for this marine resource.

Identification: Nori stands out from many seaweeds with its distinctive papery texture. In its dry state, its thin sheets feel somewhat rough, almost like fine sandpaper. However, when wet or submerged in water, it adopts a slippery smoothness, maintaining its structure without disintegrating easily. Its deep, dark green hue—almost black when underwater—lightens only slightly upon drying, signaling its rich nutrient profile, including a high concentration of chlorophyll. It's important to approach seaweeds that are too light or faded with caution, as they may not be genuine nori or they might be of lower quality. A hallmark of nori is its unexpected resilience despite its thin composition. It's this thinness that, when held against the light, gives it a mild translucence, distinguishing it from its thicker, opaque counterparts. Observing the slightly wavy edges of nori also aids in its identification, setting it apart from seaweeds with curly or excessively frilly borders. This seaweed grows naturally in large, overlapping sheets, a unique growth pattern that becomes especially noticeable when spotting multiple sheets together in their marine environment.

Habitat: Nori thrives in intertidal zones and can be found attached to rocks or other hard substrates.

Range: Historically common in the Pacific coasts of Asia, especially Japan, Korea, and China. It's also found along North American Pacific coasts.

How to cook/eat: The entire leafy part of nori is edible. While it's often consumed after being dried and then rehydrated (like in sushi rolls), nori can also be eaten fresh. It can be toasted, which gives it a crisp texture and intensifies its flavors.

Kelp (Laminaria spp.)

Family: Laminariaceae

Description: Kelp is a majestic seaweed, often forming underwater forests that teem with marine life. These towering seaweeds have been a source of sustenance and utility for coastal communities for ages, particularly in regions like Northern Europe and Asia. Apart from being a dietary staple, kelp has found applications in industries, used for its thickening properties derived from alginates.

The broad, brown fronds of kelp are not just a sight to behold but are also packed with minerals, especially iodine, making it an essential dietary supplement.

Identification: Kelp is characterized by its large size and long, ribbon-like fronds that can stretch for several meters. These fronds are typically a deep brown to olive-green color, with a somewhat rubbery and tough texture. Unlike the thin sheets of nori, kelp is thick and leathery, providing it the strength to withstand strong currents. At the base, kelp anchors itself to rocky substrates using a structure called a holdfast, which may resemble a root system but doesn't absorb nutrients like plant roots. The broad blades of kelp are smooth-edged, and their surface is somewhat slimy to touch, especially when freshly harvested from the water.

Habitat: Kelp predominantly grows in cold, nutrient-rich waters, forming kelp forests in the subtidal zones. They anchor themselves to rocky sea floors and prefer areas with regular tidal movements that bring a continuous supply of nutrients.

Range: Kelp forests are prevalent in both Northern and Southern Hemisphere coasts, especially along the Pacific coasts of North and South America, Northern Europe, and parts of Asia like Japan.

How to cook/eat: Kelp is versatile and can be consumed in various forms. While it can be rehydrated and used in soups, stews, or salads, powdered kelp can be sprinkled as a seasoning due to its salty-umami flavor. Kelp can also be pickled or used as a wrap for various dishes. Cooking kelp can soften its otherwise tough texture, making it more palatable. The entire blade or frond is edible, and due to its rich iodine content, it's often recommended to consume in moderation.

Sea Lettuce (Ulva lactuca)

Family: Ulvaceae

Description: Sea Lettuce, as the name implies, bears a striking resemblance to the land-based lettuce we often see in salads, with its delicate, leafy fronds. This vibrant green seaweed is thin and translucent, flourishing in shallow waters around the world. A favorite among vegetarians and vegans, Sea Lettuce has been historically consumed by coastal communities for its mild flavor and rich nutrient content. Containing an array of vitamins and minerals, this seaweed is not just a treat for the taste buds but also a boon for health.

Identification: Sea Lettuce stands out with its bright green, translucent sheets. It's thin, but slightly crispy when dry, and can range from being small, just a few centimeters across, to much larger fronds that might reach up to 30 cm or more. Underwater, its delicate appearance might remind one of tissue paper. Its edges are smooth to slightly wavy, without any significant frilling. In its natural habitat, when the water is clear, the sunlight filtering through gives it an almost glowing appearance.

Habitat: Sea Lettuce thrives in shallow, intertidal waters, often attaching itself to rocks, shells, or other hard substrates. However, it can also be found free-floating in calm bays or estuaries.

Range: Found globally, Sea Lettuce is common in temperate waters, both in the Northern and Southern Hemispheres. Its presence is noted along coasts in Europe, North America, and parts of Asia and Oceania.

How to cook/eat: Sea Lettuce can be consumed both raw and cooked. In its raw form, it adds a refreshing, salty touch to salads. When cooked, it melts down quite a bit, so it's advisable to use generous amounts in soups, stews, or stir-fries. Its mild taste makes it a versatile ingredient. It can also be toasted lightly and crumbled over dishes for an added crunch. Just like with other seaweeds, consuming in moderation is key, given the concentrated mineral content.

Dulse (Palmaria palmata)

Family: Palmariaceae

Description: Dulse is a well-known red seaweed, often praised for its unique, slightly spicy flavor. Recognized for its deep crimson to purplish hue, this seaweed has been an integral part of the diets of many North Atlantic coastal communities for centuries. Rich in protein, fiber, and a range of essential minerals, dulse is not only a culinary delight but also a powerhouse of nutrition.

Identification: Dulse is characterized by its reddish-brown fronds which are somewhat leathery in texture. It branches out, often resembling the shape of a hand with fingers, thus giving it another common name – "red hand of Ulster". The fronds can reach lengths of up to 50 cm or more. Unlike some other seaweeds, dulse's texture remains somewhat chewy even after drying, especially in the thicker parts of the frond.

Habitat: Dulse predominantly grows in the intertidal zone of rocky seashores. It can often be found attached to rocks or, in some cases, on the stipes of larger brown seaweeds.

Range: Commonly found in the cold waters of the North Atlantic, dulse thrives along the coasts of Northern Europe and Northeastern North America. It's especially prevalent in places like Ireland, Iceland, and parts of Canada.

How to cook/eat: Dulse is versatile and can be consumed both raw or cooked. When eaten fresh, it has a chewy texture and a salty flavor. It can be toasted quickly in a dry skillet until crispy, then crumbled over salads, soups, or added to bread dough. When rehydrated, its chewy texture works well in stews, soups, or stir-fries. Dulse is also popularly ground into flakes and used as a seasoning.

Wakame (Undaria pinnatifida)

Family: Alariaceae

Description: Wakame is a brown seaweed that enjoys significant popularity, especially in East Asian cuisines. Known for its subtly sweet taste and a satiny texture, wakame is frequently featured in soups and salads. Its delicate flavor profile and rich nutritional content, which includes calcium, iodine, and omega-3 fatty acids, have propelled its global popularity.

Identification: Wakame is easily recognizable with its long, undulating fronds that taper to slim, finger-like projections. It boasts a deep green color, sometimes bordering on brown. The base of the wakame, often called the "holdfast", attaches to rocks or other substrates. A notable characteristic is the distinctive midrib that runs through the center of each frond.

Habitat: Wakame thrives in colder sea waters and is frequently found in shallow, rocky environments, particularly in the subtidal zone where it attaches itself to rocks.

Range: Native to the cold temperate coastal areas of Japan, Korea, and China, wakame has also been introduced and cultivated in New Zealand, Europe, and the USA.

How to cook/eat: Wakame expands considerably upon rehydration, so it's essential to soak it in cold water for 10-20 minutes before use. The rehydrated seaweed becomes a bright green and regains its original soft texture. It's commonly added to miso soup, salads, and stir-fries. In salads, it's often paired with cucumber or tofu and dressed with a simple mixture of vinegar, soy sauce, and sesame oil.

Irish Moss (Chondrus crispus)

Family: Gigartinaceae

Description: Irish Moss, also known as carrageen moss, is a red seaweed known for its rich mucilaginous texture. Historically, it has been valued not only as a food source but also for its medicinal properties. Today, it is prized for the thickening agent carrageenan, which is derived from the seaweed and used in various food and cosmetic industries.

Identification: Irish Moss has a fan-like shape with multiple branches that are often curled or wavy at the tips. The color can vary, ranging from greenish-yellow, through red, to a dark purple or purplish-brown when exposed to a lot of sunlight. It feels somewhat cartilaginous, and its texture is slightly crispy when dry and slippery when wet.

Habitat: This seaweed prefers rocky substrates and can be found in the intertidal to subtidal zones of cold ocean waters.

Range: Native to the Atlantic coasts of Europe and North America, Irish Moss is especially prevalent along the shores of Ireland (from which it gets its name), the United Kingdom, and the northeastern U.S.

How to cook/eat: Before consumption, Irish Moss needs to be rehydrated in water for several hours or overnight. It can be boiled and then cooled to produce a jelly-like consistency due to its natural carrageenan content. It's popularly used as a vegetarian thickening agent for soups, stews, and even in desserts. In some Caribbean cultures, it's blended with other ingredients to make a drink believed to be an aphrodisiac and a tonic for health.

★ ★ ★ ★ ★

SUBMIT A REVIEW

If you enjoyed this chapter, I would be grateful if you could support me by leaving a review of the book on Amazon. Your feedback is very valuable and inspires me!

It's very simple and only takes a few minutes:

1. Go to the "My Orders" page on Amazon and search for the book "Forager's Harvest 101".

2. Select "Write a product review".

3. Select a Star Rating.

4. Optionally, add text, photos, or videos and select Submit.

Chapter 6: Preserving Wild Edibles

The art of preserving food is a practice as ancient as civilization itself, and in the modern era, its significance holds a special place for the foraging community. Why, one might ask, do we preserve foraged foods? The answer is multilayered. Firstly, foraging, by its very nature, often yields seasonal bounty. It's a timeless dance of reaping nature's rewards when they are plentiful and then sustaining ourselves during leaner times. Thus, preservation ensures that the hard work of foraging doesn't yield merely a transient gustatory pleasure but continues to nourish us long after the season has passed. This continuity becomes a bridge, a tether to nature's cycles even when fresh forage isn't at hand. But it's not just about prolonging the lifespan of our finds; it's also about retaining the very essence of what we collect. Preservation, when done correctly, locks in the flavors and, importantly, many of the nutrients that make foraged foods such a treasure trove of health benefits. However, this understanding of nutrient retention isn't merely academic; it shapes our methods, guiding us to choose one technique over another depending on the food in question. For instance, certain wild greens might retain more of their vitamin content when frozen rather than dried, while some berries might yield more antioxidant benefits when turned into jellies or syrups. Venturing into this realm, especially for beginners, demands a blend of enthusiasm and caution. As much as we celebrate the joys of foraging and savoring nature's bounty, we must also be acutely aware of the safety precautions that preservation entails. It's a world where minor oversights can lead to significant consequences. Improper canning, for instance, can turn a jar of wild berry jam from a delightful treat into a dangerous source of foodborne illness. Just as there are edible plants that closely resemble toxic ones, there are preservation methods that might seem right but are subtly wrong for certain foods. It underscores the importance of knowledge, of knowing not just the "how" but also the "why" of preservation. For when we understand the reasons behind each step, we're not merely following rote instructions but engaging in a deeper dialogue with our foraged finds.

Drying and Dehydrating

Drying, at its core, is the process of removing moisture from foods to prevent the growth of microorganisms and decay. By reducing the water content, we create an environment where bacteria, yeasts, and molds find it hard to grow, ensuring the food remains safe and edible for a longer time. Drying doesn't only preserve, but it also concentrates flavor, often making dried foods more potent or flavorful than their fresh counterparts.

Tools and Equipment Necessary

Dehydrators: These are specialized machines that circulate warm, dry air across food to promote faster and even drying. They come with multiple trays allowing for large batches and can maintain consistent temperatures for optimal drying.

Oven: While not as efficient as dehydrators, an oven set at its lowest temperature can be used for drying. Ensure it remains slightly ajar for moisture to escape.

Sun drying: This traditional method requires only a sunny spot and good airflow. Food is laid out on clean screens or mesh trays. It's essential to bring in the food during the evening to prevent moisture from re-entering.

Air drying: This method is mainly for herbs. Simply tie bunches of herbs and hang them upside down in a warm, dry, and well-ventilated area.

Best Practices for Dehydrating Different Foods

Herbs: These should be dried at the lowest possible temperature to retain flavor and color, usually between 95°F-115°F (35°C-46°C).

Fruits: Slice them thinly and uniformly. Pre-treating with ascorbic acid (Vitamin C) or lemon juice helps retain color. Temperatures range from 135°F-145°F (57°C-63°C).

Vegetables: Most vegetables benefit from blanching before drying to halt enzyme activity. Dry them at 125°F-135°F (52°C-57°C).

Mushrooms: Clean with a brush instead of water to retain their texture. Slice them and dry at 125°F-135°F (52°C-57°C).

Storing Dried Foods

Once dried, foods should be cooled to room temperature before storing. Use airtight containers like vacuum-sealed bags, glass jars, or plastic containers with tight-fitting lids. Store them in a cool, dark, and dry place. Ensure to check them regularly for any signs of moisture or spoilage.

Canning and Bottling

Canning is a time-tested preservation method that involves placing foods in jars and heating them to eliminate the microorganisms that cause spoilage. The process begins with selecting fresh, high-quality ingredients, as any contaminants or overly ripe products can compromise the preservation. Next, the chosen food is prepared — cleaned, chopped, and sometimes pre-cooked — and packed into sterilized jars. Once packed, a liquid like water, brine, or syrup is often added to fill the spaces between food particles. Ensuring an appropriate headspace (the space between the top of the food or liquid and the top of the jar) is vital as it allows for expansion during heating and contributes to a proper seal. The jars are then sealed with self-sealing lids and screwed-on metal bands, after which they are processed by either a water bath or pressure canning to destroy spoilage organisms and inactive enzymes. On cooling, the jar lids create a vacuum seal, preventing any new bacteria from entering and preserving the contents for a prolonged period.

Water Bath vs. Pressure Canning

Water Bath Canning is suitable for high-acid foods like fruits, jams, jellies, and salsas. The jars filled with food are submerged in boiling water, ensuring they're covered by at least an inch or two of water. The boiling water heats the contents, killing off harmful bacteria. Once processed, the jars are removed and allowed to cool, which forms a vacuum seal. Pressure Canning instead, is essential for low-acid foods like most vegetables. These foods require temperatures higher than boiling water to destroy bacteria, particularly Clostridium botulinum, which leads to botulism, a deadly food-borne illness. Pressure canning achieves these higher temperatures. Jars are placed in a pressure canner, a specialized heavy pot with a locking lid and a vent for releasing steam, and the pot is filled with several inches of water. As the pot heats, steam builds, creating pressure which in turn raises the temperature. Post-processing, the pressure is slowly released, and the jars are cooled, forming a vacuum seal.

Safety Tips and Avoiding Contamination

Ensuring safety during the canning process is essential. The first line of defense against contamination is meticulous sterilization. Before they ever meet your chosen foods, jars, lids, and bands should be diligently cleaned in hot soapy water, thoroughly rinsed, and then subjected to boiling for a full ten minutes to ensure they're utterly devoid of unwanted microorganisms. Once your bounty is sealed within, it's crucial to verify the effectiveness of your efforts. You can do this by pressing the center of each cooled lid. If it springs back, it's an indication that the vacuum seal hasn't formed properly, and such jars should be promptly refrigerated and their contents consumed in short order. While it may be tempting to get creative with your canning, it's advisable to adhere strictly to recipes from trusted sources. These have been exhaustively tested to ensure safety, and even minor alterations in ingredient ratios can upset the delicate balance, potentially compromising the pH level and, by extension, the longevity and safety of the preserved food. The matter of acidity in your chosen foods is not to be taken lightly. Foods with low acidity require the more rigorous conditions of pressure canning to ensure all harmful bacteria are destroyed. Even introducing acidifiers, such as vinegar or lemon juice, to these foods doesn't necessarily make them safe for the less intense water bath canning method unless you're following a recipe that's been specifically verified for this approach. Lastly, once you've successfully sealed your jars, ensure they are stored optimally—wipe them down, label with content and date, and stash them in a cool, dark, and dry environment. But, even with all precautions in place, always remain vigilant. Before diving into your preserved delights, check for any signs of spoilage, like an unusual odor, visible mold, or effervescence. The age-old adage holds: if in doubt, throw it out. Embracing the canning process means not only capturing the vibrancy of fresh foods but also upholding the highest standards of safety every step of the way.

Freezing Foraged Foods

Preparing Foods for Freezing

After a successful foraging venture, as you hold nature's bounties in your hands, there's a vital step before committing them to the icy embrace of your freezer: preparation. Proper preparation is the foundation of long-lasting, high-quality frozen foods. Ensure your harvest is clean, removing any foreign elements like dirt, insects, or non-edible parts. Chop or slice larger items to ensure even freezing and to maximize space. Keep in mind that the fresher the food is when it's frozen, the better the quality will be when it's thawed.

Blanching

The act of blanching — briefly immersing foods into boiling water followed by a cold-water plunge — is not just culinary theater. It serves the crucial role of halting enzyme activities which can deteriorate food quality during freezing. This ensures that the food retains its color, taste, and nutritional value. To blanch effectively, bring a pot of water to a rolling boil, immerse your foraged goods for a short time (typically a few minutes, but it can vary depending on the food), and then promptly move them to ice water to cease the cooking process. Once cooled, drain and pat dry before freezing.

Vacuum Sealing vs. Traditional Freezing Bags

There's a silent adversary in the freezing world: air. Air exposure can lead to freezer burn, compromising the texture and flavor of your foraged finds. While traditional freezing bags are commonly used, vacuum sealing offers an advantage by drawing out air and sealing the food in an airtight environment. It can extend the shelf life of frozen goods, reduce freezer burn, and preserve the flavor and nutritional content. However, if vacuum sealing isn't accessible, expelling as much air as possible from traditional freezer bags will still serve well, especially for short-term storage.

Maximizing Freezer Storage

Space in the freezer is like real estate: valuable and often limited. The organization is your ally in this endeavor. Flat-freezing items on a tray before transferring them to bags can save space and prevent clumping. Group similar items together, label clearly with dates and contents, and rotate older items to the front for easy access and to ensure they're used before newer items. If you're freezing liquids like soups or sauces, remember they expand, so leave some room in the container to accommodate this.

Pickling and Fermenting

When it comes to preserving the treasures of a foraging expedition, pickling and fermenting stand out as methods steeped in history and culinary tradition. Both harness the power of natural processes to prolong the life of food, while also elevating its flavors and enhancing its nutritional profile.

Pickling is a preservation method that employs an acidic solution, usually vinegar, to create an environment inhospitable to the microbes that spoil food. This age-old technique not only enhances the longevity of your foraged finds but also imparts a unique, tangy flavor that can be adjusted based on the spices and herbs added to the pickling solution. Over the years, pickling has transformed from a mere preservation necessity to an art form, with countless variations and recipes to suit every palate. On the other hand, fermentation relies on beneficial bacteria to convert sugars into acid, alcohol, or gases. This natural transformation results in foods like the spicy Korean kimchi or the tangy German sauerkraut, both packed with probiotics and health benefits. Whereas pickling uses an added acid to preserve, fermentation generates its own preserving agent. This wondrous alchemy means that the food not only lasts longer but is enriched with flavors that are both complex and deeply satisfying.

Equipment and Ingredients

The beauty of pickling and fermenting lies in their simplicity. Basic equipment includes clean jars with airtight lids, which can be sterilized by boiling them for 10 minutes. Weights are often used in fermentation to keep the food submerged in its liquid, ensuring an anaerobic environment where the right bacteria can thrive. Key ingredients encompass fresh produce, salt (preferably without anti-caking agents), and for pickling, vinegar with a minimum acidity of 5%. The type of water used is also crucial; chlorine-free water is best as chlorine can inhibit fermentation.

Pickling Process

Let's begin with a fundamental aspect of this preservation technique: sterilizing the jars and lids. While I recommend using new containers, it's crucial to sterilize them by boiling for at least 10-15 minutes to eliminate any bacteria.

For the brine, you'll need vinegar, water, salt, and optionally, sugar (as not all recipes call for it). Combine these ingredients in a saucepan and heat on medium-high until the salt and sugar (if used) are fully dissolved. Once done, turn off the heat and let the brine cool.

After cooling, place your foraged items in the jars. If desired, add spices or herbs such as dill, garlic, mustard seeds, peppercorns, coriander seeds, and bay leaves to enhance the flavor. Then, pour the brine over the pickels, ensuring they are fully submerged. After sealing the jars, boil them to create a vacuum seal. This step not only extends storage life but also prevents harmful bacterial growth inside the jar.

Finally, remove the jars from the heat, allow them to cool, and store in a cool, dark place. It's best to let the pickles mature for several weeks to achieve optimal flavor.

Fermenting Process

After thoroughly cleaning your foraged, the next step is salting. This crucial process acts as a deterrent to harmful bacteria while promoting the growth of beneficial ones, notably lactic acid bacteria. You can either mix the plants directly with salt or soak them in a salt solution. Typically, a salt concentration of 2 to 3 percent is used, whether based on the water for brining or the plant contents themselves. Once salted, tightly pack the plant materials into a fermentation vessel, such as a jar, ensuring they remain submerged beneath their own juices or the added brine. Minimizing air pockets is vital because exposure to air can lead to mold growth or the proliferation of unwanted bacteria. If needed, use a fermentation weight or stone to keep the plants submerged. After packing, cover the vessel, preferably with a cloth or a lid designed to let gases escape while preventing contaminants from entering.

Store the packed vessel in a cool, dark place, ideally at room temperature, around 60-70°F or 15-21°C. The fermentation duration can span anywhere from a few days to several months, contingent on the plant type and your flavor preferences. Indicators of active fermentation include bubbling, a shift from clear to a cloudier liquid, and a tangy scent.

Periodically monitoring the fermentation process is advisable. Ensure the plants stay submerged and be on the lookout for signs of spoilage. If a whitish layer of surface or kahm yeast appears, it can be skimmed off. While not detrimental, its presence might alter the final taste. Tasting helps gauge when the fermentation achieves the desired flavor and texture. Once you're satisfied, seal the jars and relocate them to a refrigerator or cold cellar, halting further fermentation. This method allows fermented plants to be preserved for months, their flavors continually evolving and deepening. Throughout the fermentation, trust your senses; if something seems amiss in appearance, scent, or texture, it's prudent to discard it.

Common Challenges and Solutions

Like any craft, pickling and fermenting come with their set of challenges. For instance, if your fermented foods become too slimy, it might be due to an overabundance of a specific bacteria or a too-high temperature during fermentation. Ensuring you maintain a consistent, cool temperature and using the right amount of salt can help mitigate this. Another challenge is the development of mold. While the top layer can be skimmed off in some cases, if mold permeates the jar, it's safest to discard the contents. Remember, while fermentation thrives in an anaerobic environment, mold requires oxygen, so keeping your produce submerged is vital. Always trust your senses; if something smells off or has an unpleasant taste, it's better to err on the side of caution and discard it.

Special Preparations

Syrups, Jams, and Jellies

Transforming foraged fruits and berries into syrups, jams, and jellies is a delightful way to capture the essence of the seasons. Start with freshly foraged, perfectly ripe, and unblemished fruits. For syrups, simmer fruits with equal parts water and sugar until they break down, then strain to achieve a clear liquid which can be stored in sterilized bottles. Jams involve a thicker consistency, incorporating both the pulp and juice of the fruit. Here, pectin — a natural gelling agent found in many fruits — plays a critical role. Some fruits, like apples and blackberries, are naturally high in pectin, while others might require an added source. The cooking process involves simmering fruit, sugar, and pectin, if needed, until it reaches a thick, spreadable consistency. Jellies, on the other hand, are made using only the juice of the fruit, resulting in a clear, bright preserve. After extracting the juice, it's combined with sugar and boiled until it reaches the gelling point. Once done, all these delicious concoctions should be poured into sterilized jars and sealed while hot, ensuring a longer shelf life.

Herbal Infusions and Teas

Harnessing the aromatic and therapeutic qualities of foraged herbs, flowers, and leaves in infusions and teas reconnects us with ancient traditions. Begin by selecting fresh, undamaged specimens, and remember to positively identify any wild plants before consumption. For an infusion, simply pour boiling water over your chosen herbs and let them steep for about 5-10 minutes, depending on the plant's nature and personal preference. This method is especially useful for delicate parts like flowers or leaves. Teas require a slightly longer process, often involving drying the foraged item first. Once dried, they can be steeped in hot water for several minutes to extract their flavors and beneficial properties. To dry herbs for tea, tie them in small bundles and hang them upside down in a warm, airy location away from direct sunlight. When completely dried, store them in airtight containers to retain their potency and aroma.

Spirits and Beverages

The world of foraged spirits and beverages is vast and exhilarating, with opportunities to create unique drinks that capture the soul of the wild. From berry-infused vodkas to pine needle gins, the base process usually involves steeping foraged items in a chosen spirit to impart flavors. Start by ensuring that the chosen botanicals are clean and free of pesticides or contaminants. Place them into a sterilized jar and pour over your spirit of choice, ensuring that they are fully submerged. The infusion period can range from a few days to several weeks, depending on the intensity of flavor desired. After the infusion, strain the spirit and bottle it. Remember, alcoholic infusions extract both flavors and potential toxins, so be extra cautious about plant identification. For non-alcoholic beverages, think of fermented drinks like elderflower champagne or dandelion beer. Here, the natural yeast present on plants aids in the fermentation process, creating carbonated and flavorsome beverages that are a testament to the richness of nature.

Storage Tips and Shelf Life

Regardless of the preparation method, storage plays a crucial role in maintaining the quality of your foraged creations. A cool, dry place away from direct sunlight works best for most preserves. For liquid concoctions, like syrups and spirits, ensuring airtight sealing and refrigeration (post-opening) can significantly extend shelf life. As with any preserved food, always check for signs of spoilage before consumption.

Organizing and Labelling

As with any culinary or preservation endeavor, the efforts of foraging can quickly become overwhelmed by disorganization. The transition from nature's wild abundance to the systematic confines of your pantry, refrigerator, or freezer is pivotal in ensuring that your foraged treasures are savored and not wasted. Central to this transition is the art of organization and the precision of labeling.

Each jar, container, or bag from the outdoors carries within it a snapshot of a season, a moment of time when nature was in a particular bloom. But time, temperature, and external factors can affect its longevity. To get the best from stored foods, it's essential to regularly check for signs of spoilage or deterioration. Changes in color, an off-putting aroma, or a change in texture can often be the first indicators. Maintaining a cool, dark environment for most preserved goods will aid in retaining their freshness. Rotating your stock, so older items are used first, can also be beneficial. This process, often termed 'First In, First Out', ensures that items don't remain stored beyond their prime.

Despite the best of intentions and methods, one might occasionally encounter issues in storage. Mold is a common antagonist, often appearing when there's been an introduction of unwanted bacteria or when the storage environment is too humid. If spotted early, mold on hard cheeses or firm vegetables can be removed, but moldy preserves, bread, or soft fruits should be discarded. Another issue, especially with canned goods, is the unsealing of jars, which might indicate a change in pressure or a possible contamination. Jars with bulging lids, or those that give off an unusual odor upon opening, should be discarded without tasting.

Recognizing the typical shelf life of different preserved items becomes paramount. Dried goods, like herbs or mushrooms, can last for several months to a year when stored in a cool, dark place. Canned or bottled goods, if processed correctly, can last even longer, often up to a year or more. Freezed items, depending on the efficiency of the freezer and the nature of the food, can range from a month (for items like bread) to a year (for meats or blanched vegetables). Labeling containers with both the date of preservation and an estimated 'best by' date can alleviate the guesswork. With a clear understanding of each item's temporal journey and a well-organized system in place, one can maximize the enjoyment of foraged foods while minimizing waste and potential health risks.

SUBMIT A REVIEW

If you enjoyed this chapter, I would be grateful if you could support me by leaving a review of the book on Amazon. Your feedback is very valuable and inspires me!

It's very simple and only takes a few minutes:

1. Go to the "My Orders" page on Amazon and search for the book "Forager's Harvest 101".

2. Select "Write a product review".

3. Select a Star Rating.

4. Optionally, add text, photos, or videos and select Submit.

Chapter 7: Recipes

Breakfast, Snacks and More (For Two)

Serviceberry Pancakes

Ingredients:

- 1 cup all-purpose flour
- 2 tbsp sugar
- 1 tsp baking powder
- 1/2 tsp baking soda
- 1/4 tsp salt
- 1/2 cup milk
- 1/2 cup buttermilk
- 1 large egg
- 2 tbsp melted butter
- 1/2 cup fresh serviceberries (Amechanlier spp.)
- Butter or oil for cooking

Instructions:

Begin by combining the all-purpose flour, sugar, baking powder, baking soda, and salt in a mixing bowl. In a separate bowl, whisk together the milk, buttermilk, egg, and melted butter until well-blended. Now, merge the wet and dry ingredients, taking care not to overmix; a few lumps in the batter are acceptable. Gently incorporate the fresh serviceberries into the batter. Heat a griddle or skillet over medium heat and lightly grease it with butter or oil. Pour approximately 1/4 cup of batter onto the griddle for each pancake. Allow the pancakes to cook until bubbles form on the surface, then carefully flip them and cook until both sides achieve a desirable golden brown hue. Repeat the process with the remaining batter, generating a stack of delightful pancakes. Serve the pancakes warm, accompanied by a drizzle of maple syrup or a topping of your choice.

Wild Strawberry and Raspberry Smoothie

Ingredients:

- 2 cups wild strawberries (Fragaria virginiana)
- 1 cup raspberries (Rubus spp.)
- 2 bananas, peeled and sliced
- 1 cup Greek yogurt
- 1 cup almond milk
- 2 tbsp honey (optional)
- Ice cubes

Instructions:

Begin by assembling 2 cups of fresh wild strawberries and combining them with 1 cup of raspberries. Integrate 2 peeled and sliced bananas for a creamy element. Incorporate 1 cup of Greek yogurt and 1 cup of almond milk to enhance the body and flavor profile. If desired, add 2 tablespoons of honey for a touch of sweetness. Transfer the amalgamation to a blender and add ice cubes. Blend until the texture is smooth.

Riverbank Grape Jam on Toast

Ingredients:

- 1 cup riverbank grapes (Vitis riparia), washed and stemmed
- 1/2 cup sugar
- 1 tbsp lemon juice
- 4 slices whole grain bread
- Butter, for spreading

Instructions:

Begin by washing and stemming 1 cup of riverbank grapes. In a pot, combine the grapes, 1/2 cup of sugar, and 1 tablespoon of lemon juice. Heat the mixture over medium-low heat, stirring occasionally, until the grapes release their juices and the sugar dissolves. Once the grapes have softened and the mixture thickens, use a potato masher or a fork to gently crush the grapes and break them down further. Continue simmering until the jam reaches your desired consistency. While the jam is simmering, toast 4 slices of whole grain bread until they are golden and crisp. Once the jam has thickened to your liking, remove it from the heat and let it cool slightly. Spread a layer of butter on each slice of toasted bread, and then generously spread the riverbank grape jam on top.

Blueberry and Maple Syrup Compote

Ingredients:

- 1 cup blueberries
- 2 tablespoons maple syrup
- 1/2 teaspoon lemon zest
- 1 teaspoon lemon juice
- Pinch of cinnamon (optional)

Instructions:

Start by rinsing and draining 1 cup of fresh blueberries. In a small saucepan, combine the blueberries, 2 tablespoons of maple syrup, 1/2 teaspoon of lemon zest, and 1 teaspoon of lemon juice. If desired, add a pinch of cinnamon to enhance the flavor profile. Place the saucepan over low to medium heat, gently simmering the mixture. Stir occasionally and let the blueberries release their juices, creating a luscious compote. Continue to simmer the compote for about 5-7 minutes, or until the blueberries soften and the mixture thickens slightly. Once the compote reaches your desired consistency, remove it from the heat. Serve the Blueberry and Maple Syrup Compote warm, spooned over pancakes, waffles, yogurt, or desserts.

Dandelion Root Coffee

Ingredients:

- 2 tablespoons roasted dandelion root
- 2 cups water
- Milk or cream, to taste (optional)
- Sweetener, to taste (optional)

Instructions:

Begin by acquiring 2 tablespoons of roasted dandelion root, which is commonly available as a coffee substitute. In a pot, bring 2 cups of water to a boil. Add the roasted dandelion root to the boiling water. Reduce the heat to low and let the mixture simmer for about 5-10 minutes, allowing the flavors to infuse. Once the dandelion root has steeped to your liking, strain the liquid into cups, discarding the used dandelion root. If desired, add a splash of milk or cream to your preference for a creamier texture. For additional sweetness, stir in your choice of sweetener to suit your taste.

Wild Ginger and Blackberry Sorbet

Ingredients:

- 2 cups blackberries (Rubus spp.)
- 1 tablespoon wild ginger (Asarum canadense), finely chopped
- 1/2 cup water
- 1/4 cup sugar
- 1 tablespoon lemon juice

Instructions:

Begin by washing and draining 2 cups of fresh blackberries. In a small saucepan, combine 1/2 cup of water and 1/4 cup of sugar. Heat over medium heat, stirring until the sugar dissolves. Let the mixture cool. Place the blackberries and 1 tablespoon of finely chopped wild ginger in a blender. Pour in the cooled sugar syrup and 1 tablespoon of lemon juice. Blend the mixture until smooth, creating a fragrant base for the sorbet. Pour the blended mixture into a shallow dish, such as a baking pan. Place it in the freezer. Every 30 minutes, use a fork to scrape and mix the partially frozen sorbet. Continue this process for about 2-3 hours, until the sorbet reaches a smooth and scoopable consistency. Serve the Wild Ginger and Blackberry Sorbet in chilled bowls for a refreshing dessert.

Serviceberry Cobbler

Ingredients:

For the Filling:

- 2 cups fresh serviceberries (Amelanchier spp.)
- 1/4 cup granulated sugar
- 1 tablespoon cornstarch
- 1 tablespoon lemon juice
- 1/2 cup all-purpose flour
- 2 tablespoons granulated sugar
- 1/2 teaspoon baking powder
- 1/8 teaspoon salt
- 2 tablespoons cold unsalted butter, cubed
- 3 tablespoons milk

Instructions:

Start by preheating your oven to 375°F (190°C). In a bowl, combine 2 cups of fresh serviceberries, 1/4 cup of granulated sugar, 1 tablespoon of cornstarch, and 1 tablespoon of lemon juice. Toss the ingredients together until the serviceberries are well coated. Transfer the berry mixture into a small baking dish suitable for two servings. For the topping, in a separate bowl, whisk together 1/2 cup of all-purpose flour, 2 tablespoons of granulated sugar, 1/2 teaspoon of baking powder, and 1/8 teaspoon of salt. Add 2 tablespoons of cold, cubed unsalted butter to the dry mixture. Use a pastry cutter or your fingers to work the butter into the flour until the mixture resembles coarse crumbs. Pour in 3 tablespoons of milk and stir until the mixture just comes together to form a dough. Drop spoonfuls of the dough evenly over the serviceberry filling in the baking dish. Bake the cobbler in the preheated oven for about 25-30 minutes, or until the topping is golden brown and the filling is bubbly. Once baked, remove the cobbler from the oven and let it cool slightly before serving.

Salads (For Two)

Ramps and Wild Strawberry Salad

Ingredients:

- Fresh ramps (Allium tricoccum), prepared
- 1 cup wild strawberries (Fragaria virginiana), halved
- 1/4 cup crumbled cheese (like goat cheese, feta or parmesan)

- 2 tbsp toasted pine nuts
- 2 tbsp extra virgin olive oil
- 1 tbsp balsamic vinegar
- Salt and pepper, to taste

Instructions:

Begin by preparing fresh ramps. In a bowl, combine the ramps and halved wild strawberries. Sprinkle the crumbled cheese and toasted pine nuts over the mixture. In a separate bowl, whisk together the extra virgin olive oil, balsamic vinegar, salt, and pepper. Drizzle the dressing over the salad and give it a gentle toss to evenly coat the ingredients. Serve promptly.

Watercress and Wood Sorrel Salad

Ingredients:

- 2 cups watercress
- 1 cup wood sorrel (Oxalis acetosella)
- 1/4 cup crumbled cheese (like goat cheese, feta or parmesan)
- 2 tbsp toasted walnuts, chopped
- 2 tbsp olive oil
- 1 tbsp lemon juice
- Salt and pepper, to taste

Instructions:

Begin by thoroughly washing and drying 2 cups of watercress leaves. Place them in a salad bowl. Add 1 cup of wood sorrel leaves to the bowl, enhancing the mix with their tangy undertones. Sprinkle 1/4 cup of crumbled cheese over the greens. To elevate the texture, scatter 2 tablespoons of chopped toasted walnuts across the salad. In a separate container, whisk together 2 tablespoons of olive oil and 1 tablespoon of lemon juice. Season the dressing with a pinch of salt and a dash of pepper. Drizzle the dressing over the salad and toss gently to evenly coat the ingredients with the vibrant flavors.

Dandelion and Raspberry Salad

Ingredients:

- 4 cups fresh dandelion greens
- 1 cup raspberries (Rubus spp.)
- 1/4 cup crumbled cheese (like goat cheese, feta or parmesan)
- 2 tbsp chopped walnuts
- 2 tbsp olive oil
- 1 tbsp balsamic vinegar
- 1 tsp honey
- Salt and pepper, to taste

Instructions:

Begin by washing and drying 4 cups of fresh dandelion greens. Place them in a salad bowl. Add 1 cup of raspberries to the bowl, introducing a burst of vibrant sweetness. Sprinkle 1/4 cup of crumbled cheese over the greens, offering a creamy contrast to the sharpness of the dandelion leaves. To enrich the texture, scatter 2 tablespoons of chopped walnuts across the salad. In a separate container, whisk together 2 tablespoons of olive oil, 1 tablespoon of balsamic vinegar, and 1 teaspoon of honey. Season the dressing with a pinch of salt and a dash of pepper. Drizzle the dressing over the salad and gently toss to ensure an even coating of the ingredients with the lively flavors.

Cattail and Avocado Salad

Ingredients:

- 2 cups young cattail shoots, cleaned and sliced
- 1 ripe avocado, diced
- 1 cup cherry tomatoes, halved
- 1/4 cup red onion, thinly sliced
- 1/4 cup crumbled cheese (like goat cheese, feta or parmesan)
- Fresh herbs (such as parsley or chives), chopped
- 3 tablespoons olive oil
- 1 tablespoon lemon juice
- 1 teaspoon Dijon mustard
- 1 clove garlic, minced
- Salt and pepper, to taste

Instructions:

In a bowl, combine 2 cups of cleaned and sliced young cattail shoots, 1 diced ripe avocado, 1 cup of halved cherry tomatoes, and 1/4 cup of thinly sliced red onion. Sprinkle 1/4 cup of crumbled cheese over the salad, adding a creamy and tangy element. Add a handful of chopped fresh herbs, such as parsley or chives, for an aromatic touch. Season the salad with salt and pepper to enhance the flavors. In a separate small bowl, whisk together 3 tablespoons of olive oil, 1 tablespoon of lemon juice, 1 teaspoon of Dijon mustard, 1 minced clove of garlic, and a pinch of salt and pepper to create a zesty dressing. Drizzle the dressing over the salad and gently toss to coat all the ingredients evenly.

Main Courses (For Two)

Maple-Raspberry Glazed Chicken

Ingredients:

- 2 chicken breasts
- 3 tbsp maple syrup
- 2 tbsp crushed raspberries
- 1 tbsp olive oil
- Salt and pepper

Optional: Fresh raspberries and herbs for garnish

Instructions:

In a bowl, create the glaze by mixing together 3 tablespoons of maple syrup and 2 tablespoons of crushed raspberries. Add a pinch of salt and a dash of pepper to the mixture. Coat the 2 chicken breasts generously with the prepared glaze, ensuring they are evenly covered. Allow the chicken to marinate in the refrigerator for approximately 30 minutes. Heat 1 tablespoon of olive oil in a skillet over medium heat. Once the skillet is hot, add the marinated chicken breasts. Cook each side for about 6-7 minutes, or until they achieve a golden-brown hue and are fully cooked through. During the last moments of cooking, pour the remaining glaze over the chicken breasts, creating an additional layer of flavor. Transfer the cooked chicken breasts to serving plates. For an extra touch, consider garnishing with fresh raspberries and a sprinkle of your preferred herbs. Serve the Maple-Raspberry Glazed Chicken hot, accompanied by wild rice or a side salad.

Groundnut and Wild Ginger Soup

Ingredients:

- 1 cup groundnut (Apios americana), peeled and chopped
- 1/4 cup wild ginger (Asarum canadense), finely chopped
- 1 onion, chopped
- 2 cloves garlic, minced
- 2 cups vegetable broth
- 1 cup potatoes, peeled and diced
- 1/2 cup carrots, peeled and diced
- 1/2 cup celery, diced
- 2 tbsp olive oil
- Salt and pepper, to taste

Instructions:

Commence by heating olive oil in a pot over medium heat. Add chopped onion and minced garlic, sautéing until translucent. Introduce the peeled and diced groundnut, allowing it to infuse with the aromatic base. Incorporate the diced potatoes, carrots, and celery. Pour in vegetable broth, elevating the composition, and allowing it to simmer until the components meld harmoniously. Now, introduce the finely chopped wild ginger. Season with salt and pepper to achieve a balanced resonance of flavors. As the ingredients harmonize, transfer the mixture to a blender. Blend until smooth. Return the blended concoction to the pot, reheating gently if needed.

Sautéed Fiddleheads with Ramp

Ingredients:

- 2 cups fiddlehead ferns
- 1 cup fresh ramps (Allium tricoccum), bulbs and leaves separated
- 2 tbsp butter
- 1 tbsp olive oil
- Salt and pepper, to taste
- Lemon wedges, for serving (optional)

Instructions:

Begin by cleaning and trimming 2 cups of fiddlehead ferns, removing any tough ends. Wash them thoroughly and set aside. Separate the bulbs and leaves of the fresh ramps. Finely chop the bulbs and set aside. Slice the leaves into thin strips and set them aside as well. In a skillet, heat 2 tablespoons of butter and 1 tablespoon of olive oil over medium heat. Add the chopped ramp bulbs and sauté until they become tender and translucent. Introduce the cleaned fiddlehead ferns into the skillet, ensuring they are in a single layer. Sauté for a few minutes until they start to brown, shaking the skillet occasionally for even cooking. Incorporate the sliced ramp leaves into the skillet, gently tossing to combine with the fiddleheads. Season the mixture with salt and pepper according to your taste. Once the fiddleheads are tender and vibrant in color, remove the skillet from heat. Serve the sautéed fiddleheads and ramps as a side dish, optionally accompanied by lemon wedges for a touch of brightness.

Purslane Stir-Fry

Ingredients:

- 2 cups purslane (Portulaca oleracea), washed and chopped
- 1 onion, thinly sliced
- 1 bell pepper, thinly sliced
- 1 carrot, julienned
- 2 cloves garlic, minced
- 2 tbsp soy sauce
- 1 tbsp sesame oil
- 1 tsp ginger, grated
- 1 tsp red pepper flakes (optional)
- Salt and pepper, to taste

Instructions:

Begin by washing and chopping 2 cups of purslane, setting it aside. Heat a pan over medium-high heat and add a drizzle of oil. Sauté 1 thinly sliced onion until it turns translucent. Introduce 1 thinly sliced bell pepper and 1 julienned carrot to the pan. Stir-fry until they achieve a tender-crisp texture. Add 2 minced cloves of garlic and 1 teaspoon of grated ginger to the pan. If desired, incorporate 1 teaspoon of red pepper flakes for a touch of heat. Gently fold in the chopped purslane, allowing it to wilt and become incorporated with the other ingredients. Pour 2 tablespoons of soy sauce and 1 tablespoon of sesame oil over the stir-fry, ensuring an even distribution of flavors. Season with salt and pepper according to your taste. Continue to stir-fry for a few more minutes until all the components are well combined and heated through.

Cattail and Wild Rice Soup

Ingredients:

- 1 cup wild rice
- 4 cups vegetable broth
- 2 cups cattail shoots, cleaned and chopped
- 1 onion, diced
- 2 carrots, peeled and diced
- 2 celery stalks, diced

- 2 cloves garlic, minced
- 2 tablespoons olive oil
- Salt and pepper, to taste
- Fresh parsley, for garnish (optional)

Instructions:

In a pot, combine 1 cup of wild rice and 4 cups of vegetable broth. Bring to a boil, then reduce the heat to low, cover, and let the rice simmer for about 40-45 minutes, or until tender and fully cooked. Set aside. Heat 2 tablespoons of olive oil in a separate pot over medium heat. Add the diced onion, carrots, and celery. Sauté until the vegetables become softened and the onion turns translucent. Introduce 2 cloves of minced garlic to the pot, stirring for about 1 minute until fragrant. Add the cleaned and chopped cattail shoots to the pot, allowing them to cook alongside the vegetables for a few minutes. Pour in the cooked wild rice, blending it with the mixture in the pot. Gradually add the vegetable broth, adjusting the amount to achieve your preferred consistency. Simmer the soup for an additional 10-15 minutes, allowing the flavors to meld. Season the soup with salt and pepper according to your taste. Once the soup is ready, ladle it into bowls. For a touch of vibrancy, garnish with fresh parsley if desired.

Wild Rice and Groundnut Pilaf

Ingredients:

- 1/2 cup wild rice
- 1/4 cup groundnut (Apios americana), peeled and chopped
- 1/4 cup onion, finely chopped
- 1/4 cup carrot, finely diced
- 1/4 cup celery, finely diced
- 2 tbsp olive oil
- 1 1/4 cups vegetable broth
- Salt and pepper, to taste

Instructions:

Start by rinsing 1/2 cup of wild rice under cold water. Drain and set aside. In a pot, heat 2 tablespoons of olive oil over medium heat. Add 1/4 cup of finely chopped onion and sauté until translucent. Stir in 1/4 cup of finely diced carrot and 1/4 cup of finely diced celery, cooking for a few minutes until they begin to soften. Add the chopped groundnut to the pot and sauté for another 2-3 minutes, allowing the flavors to meld. Introduce the rinsed wild rice to the pot and stir well, coating the rice and vegetables with the aromatic mixture. Pour in 1 1/4 cups of vegetable broth, elevating the flavors of the pilaf. Season with salt and pepper according to your taste. Bring the mixture to a boil, then reduce the heat to low. Cover the pot and let the pilaf simmer for about 40-45 minutes, or until the wild rice is tender and has absorbed the liquid. Once the pilaf is cooked, fluff it gently with a fork to separate the grains.

Dandelion and Egg Frittata

Ingredients:

- 4 large eggs
- 1 cup fresh dandelion greens, washed and chopped

- 1/2 cup wild onion bulbs (Allium spp.), finely chopped
- 1/4 cup crumbled cheese (like goat cheese, feta or parmesan)
- 2 tablespoons olive oil
- Salt and pepper, to taste

Instructions:

Crack 4 eggs into a bowl. In a skillet, heat 2 tablespoons of olive oil over medium heat. Add 1/2 cup of finely chopped wild onion bulbs and sauté until they become tender and aromatic. Introduce 1 cup of chopped dandelion greens to the skillet. Sauté for a few minutes until they wilt and reduce in volume. Pour the beaten eggs over the sautéed vegetables, ensuring an even distribution. Sprinkle 1/4 cup of crumbled cheese over the mixture, adding a creamy and tangy layer to the frittata. Season the frittata with salt and pepper to taste. Allow the frittata to cook undisturbed for a few minutes until the edges set. Transfer the skillet to a preheated oven under the broiler for a couple of minutes until the top is golden and the eggs are fully cooked. Slide the finished Dandelion and Egg Frittata onto a cutting board. Slice it into wedges and serve warm.

Fiddlehead and Wild Salmon Stir-Fry

Ingredients:

- 2 wild salmon fillets
- 1 cup fiddleheads, cleaned and trimmed
- 1 red bell pepper, thinly sliced
- 1 carrot, julienned
- 2 tablespoons soy sauce
- 1 tablespoon sesame oil
- 1 tablespoon honey
- 2 cloves garlic, minced
- 1 teaspoon fresh ginger, grated
- 2 tablespoons olive oil
- Salt and pepper, to taste

Instructions:

Start by marinating 2 wild salmon fillets with 1 tablespoon of soy sauce, 1/2 tablespoon of sesame oil, and a pinch of salt and pepper. Set aside to allow the flavors to meld. Heat 2 tablespoons of olive oil in a wok or large skillet over medium-high heat. Add 1 cup of cleaned and trimmed fiddleheads to the wok. Stir-fry for about 3-4 minutes until they become tender-crisp. Introduce 1 thinly sliced red bell pepper and 1 julienned carrot to the wok. Continue stir-frying for an additional 2-3 minutes until the vegetables are vibrant and slightly softened. Clear a space in the wok and add 2 minced cloves of garlic and 1 teaspoon of grated fresh ginger. Sauté for about 30 seconds until fragrant. Push the vegetables to the side and place the marinated salmon fillets in the center of the wok. Cook for approximately 3-4 minutes on each side, or until the salmon is cooked through and flakes easily. In a small bowl, whisk together 1 tablespoon of soy sauce, 1/2 tablespoon of sesame oil, and 1 tablespoon of honey to create a savory-sweet sauce. Pour the sauce over the stir-fry and toss everything together, ensuring an even coating of the flavors.

Dandelion and Groundnut Meatballs in Sassafras Sauce

Ingredients:

- 1/2 cup ground groundnut (Apios americana)
- 1/2 cup cooked quinoa
- 1/4 cup finely chopped dandelion greens
- 1/4 cup finely chopped onion
- 1 egg
- 1/4 teaspoon ground cumin
- 1 cup vegetable broth
- 1/4 cup heavy cream
- 1 tablespoon sassafras root bark, dried and crushed
- 1 tablespoon butter
- Salt and pepper, to taste

Instructions:

In a bowl, combine 1/2 cup of ground groundnut, 1/2 cup of cooked quinoa, 1/4 cup of finely chopped dandelion greens, 1/4 cup of finely chopped onion, 1 egg, 1/4 teaspoon of ground cumin, and salt and pepper to taste. Mix the ingredients until well combined, then shape the mixture into small meatballs. In a skillet, heat a bit of oil over medium heat. Add the meatballs and cook until they are browned on all sides and cooked through. Remove the meatballs from the skillet and set them aside. In the same skillet, melt 1 tablespoon of butter. Add 1 tablespoon of dried and crushed sassafras root bark and sauté for a minute to release its flavors. Pour in 1 cup of vegetable broth and bring the mixture to a simmer. Let it cook for a few minutes to infuse the broth with the sassafras flavor. Stir in 1/4 cup of heavy cream and let the sauce simmer for a few more minutes until it thickens slightly. Season with salt and pepper to taste. Return the cooked meatballs to the skillet and coat them with the sassafras sauce.

Oyster Mushroom and Dandelion Fritters

Ingredients:

- 1 cup oyster mushrooms, cleaned and chopped
- 1/2 cup dandelion petals, cleaned and chopped
- 1/4 cup onion, finely chopped
- 1/4 cup all-purpose flour
- 1/4 cup cornmeal
- 1/2 teaspoon baking powder
- 1/4 teaspoon paprika
- 1/3 cup milk
- 1 egg
- Vegetable oil, for frying
- 1/4 cup Greek yogurt
- 1 tablespoon lemon juice

- 1 tablespoon chopped fresh herbs (such as chives or parsley)
- Salt and pepper, to taste

Instructions:

In a bowl, combine 1 cup of chopped oyster mushrooms, 1/2 cup of chopped dandelion petals, and 1/4 cup of finely chopped onion. In a separate bowl, whisk together 1/4 cup of all-purpose flour, 1/4 cup of cornmeal, 1/2 teaspoon of baking powder, 1/4 teaspoon of paprika, and a pinch of salt and pepper. In another bowl, whisk together 1/3 cup of milk and 1 egg until well blended. Pour the wet mixture into the dry mixture and stir until a batter forms. Add the mushroom, dandelion, and onion mixture to the batter. Gently fold them in until evenly distributed. Heat vegetable oil in a skillet over medium-high heat for frying. Using a spoon, carefully drop spoonful of the batter into the hot oil. Flatten slightly with the back of the spoon. Fry the fritters for about 2-3 minutes on each side, or until they are golden brown and crispy. Remove the fritters from the oil and place them on a paper towel-lined plate to drain excess oil. In a small bowl, prepare the dip by combining 1/4 cup of Greek yogurt, 1 tablespoon of lemon juice, chopped fresh herbs, salt, and pepper.

Porcino and Ramp-Stuffed Trout

Ingredients:

- 2 whole trout, cleaned and gutted
- 1/2 cup chopped porcini mushrooms
- 1/4 cup chopped ramps (Allium tricoccum)
- 1/4 cup breadcrumbs
- 2 tablespoons olive oil
- 1 lemon, sliced
- Salt and pepper, to taste
- 2 tablespoons unsalted butter, softened
- 1 tablespoon fresh herbs (such as thyme, rosemary, or parsley), chopped

Instructions:

Preheat your oven to 375°F (190°C). In a bowl, combine 1/2 cup of chopped porcini mushrooms, 1/4 cup of chopped ramps, 1/4 cup of breadcrumbs, 2 tablespoons of olive oil, and salt and pepper to taste. Rinse the trout and pat them dry with paper towels. Stuff the trout cavities with the mushroom and ramp mixture. In another bowl, mix 2 tablespoons of softened unsalted butter, 1 tablespoon of chopped fresh herbs, salt, and pepper. Rub the herb butter all over the outside of the stuffed trout. Place a few lemon slices inside the trout cavities and lay a couple more slices on top. Wrap each stuffed trout in aluminum foil, creating a sealed pouch. Bake the trout in the preheated oven for about 20-25 minutes, or until the fish is cooked through and flakes easily with a fork. Carefully unwrap the foil pouches and transfer the stuffed trout to serving plates.

Morels and Watercress Pasta

Ingredients:

- 8 oz pasta (such as fettuccine or linguine)
- 1 cup fresh morel mushrooms, cleaned and sliced
- 1 bunch watercress, stems removed
- 2 cloves garlic, minced

- 1/4 cup heavy cream
- 1/4 cup grated Parmesan cheese
- 2 tablespoons butter
- 2 tablespoons olive oil
- Salt and pepper, to taste

Instructions:

In a skillet, heat 2 tablespoons of butter and 2 tablespoons of olive oil over medium heat. Add 1 cup of sliced morel mushrooms and sauté until tender and lightly browned. Incorporate 2 minced cloves of garlic and sauté until fragrant. Stir in 1/4 cup of heavy cream and let it simmer briefly. Gently fold in cooked pasta, coating it with the creamy mushroom sauce. Add 1/4 cup of grated Parmesan cheese and toss to combine. Tear leaves from a bunch of watercress and add them to the pasta. Toss until the watercress slightly wilts. Season with salt and pepper.

Shaggy Mane and Purslane Stir-Fry

Ingredients:

- 2 cups shaggy mane mushrooms, cleaned and sliced
- 1 cup purslane leaves, cleaned and chopped
- 1/2 cup red bell pepper, thinly sliced
- 1/2 cup onion, thinly sliced
- 2 cloves garlic, minced
- 2 tablespoons vegetable oil
- Salt and pepper, to taste
- 2 tablespoons soy sauce
- 1 tablespoon rice vinegar
- 1 tablespoon honey
- 1 teaspoon sesame oil
- 1/2 teaspoon fresh ginger, grated
- 1/2 teaspoon cornstarch (optional, for thickening)

Instructions:

In a small bowl, whisk together 2 tablespoons of soy sauce, 1 tablespoon of rice vinegar, 1 tablespoon of honey, 1 teaspoon of sesame oil, and 1/2 teaspoon of grated fresh ginger to create the stir-fry sauce. If you prefer a thicker sauce, you can add 1/2 teaspoon of cornstarch to the mixture and whisk until well combined. Heat 2 tablespoons of vegetable oil in a wok or large skillet over high heat. Add 2 cups of sliced shaggy mane mushrooms, 1/2 cup of thinly sliced red bell pepper, and 1/2 cup of thinly sliced onion to the hot oil. Stir-fry for a few minutes until the vegetables start to soften and the mushrooms release their moisture. Stir in 2 cloves of minced garlic and continue to stir-fry for about 30 seconds until fragrant. Add 1 cup of chopped purslane leaves to the wok and toss everything together. Pour the prepared stir-fry sauce over the mushroom and vegetable mixture. Stir-fry for an additional 1-2 minutes, allowing the sauce to coat all the ingredients and thicken slightly. Season the Shaggy Mane and Purslane Stir-Fry with salt and pepper to taste.

Porcino-Stuffed Chicken with Groundnut Sauce

Ingredients:

- 2 boneless, skinless chicken breasts
- 1/2 cup chopped porcini mushrooms
- 1/4 cup chopped onion
- 1/4 cup breadcrumbs
- 2 tablespoons olive oil
- 1/4 cup ground groundnut (Apios americana)
- 1 cup chicken broth
- 2 tablespoons butter
- 1 tablespoon all-purpose flour
- Salt and pepper, to taste

Instructions:

Preheat the oven to 375°F (190°C). In a bowl, combine 1/2 cup of chopped porcini mushrooms, 1/4 cup of chopped onion, 1/4 cup of breadcrumbs, 2 tablespoons of olive oil, and salt and pepper to taste. Carefully butterfly the chicken breasts by slicing them horizontally, leaving one edge uncut to create a pocket. Stuff each chicken breast with the porcini mixture, then secure the pockets with toothpicks. In an oven-safe skillet, heat a bit of oil over medium-high heat. Sear the stuffed chicken breasts for a few minutes on each side until golden brown. Transfer the skillet to the preheated oven and bake for about 15-20 minutes, or until the chicken is cooked through. While the chicken is baking, prepare the groundnut sauce. In a small saucepan, melt 2 tablespoons of butter. Add 1 tablespoon of all-purpose flour and cook for a minute to create a roux. Gradually whisk in 1 cup of chicken broth and bring the mixture to a simmer. Stir in 1/4 cup of ground groundnut and let the sauce simmer until it thickens. Season with salt and pepper to taste. Once the chicken is done baking, remove the toothpicks and slice each stuffed breast.

⭐ ⭐ ⭐ ⭐ ⭐

SUBMIT A REVIEW

If you enjoyed this chapter, I would be grateful if you could support me by leaving a review of the book on Amazon. Your feedback is very valuable and inspires me!

It's very simple and only takes a few minutes:

1. Go to the "My Orders" page on Amazon and search for the book "Forager's Harvest 101".

2. Select "Write a product review".

3. Select a Star Rating.

4. Optionally, add text, photos, or videos and select Submit.

Chapter 8: Foraging as A Lifestyle

Foraging, the age-old practice of sourcing wild foods directly from their natural habitats, has witnessed a resurgence in modern times, not just as a hobby but as a potent avenue for sustainable living. At the heart of this lifestyle is the emphasis on local and seasonal eating. Consuming foods that sprout in your vicinity and are available for that particular time of year is not only a culinary delight but also an environmental boon. When foods are sourced locally, we drastically cut down on the carbon emissions that arise from transporting foods over vast distances. The miles that a single apple or bunch of spinach might travel to reach your plate from another continent are startling, each mile adding to the environmental cost. Foraging eliminates these "food miles," ensuring that what graces our plate has often been plucked a few miles, if not a few steps, away.

Beyond the carbon savings, foraging imparts another sustainable advantage: a dramatic reduction in waste. Unlike supermarket veggies where we might discard leaves, stems, or imperfect parts, foraging instills a deep appreciation for the entirety of the plant. Root to stem, foragers find uses for parts of plants that might traditionally be considered waste. This approach not only means maximizing the culinary potential of a plant but also ensures that little is left behind, reducing the volume of food waste that contributes to landfills and ensuing methane emissions.

Delving deeper into the rhythms of foraging, one can't help but notice the profound cyclical connection it fosters. It's a dance that aligns with nature's own cycles. As the seasons shift, so does the palette of offerings in the wild. Spring might usher in tender greens and blossoms, summer might burst with berries, autumn might present a medley of mushrooms, and even winter, with its stark landscape, might offer hidden roots and barks. Engaging with this ever-changing array ensures that foragers are in tune with the rhythms of the earth, only taking what nature can afford to give at any given time. This approach not only ensures ecological balance but also actively promotes biodiversity. Instead of focusing on a few cultivated crops, foragers celebrate a wide spectrum of species, many of which might be overlooked in commercial agriculture.

Speaking of commercial agriculture, it's impossible to ignore the mounting challenges it faces. Today's large-scale farming often revolves around monocultures—expanses of land dedicated to growing a single crop. This lack of diversity can render ecosystems vulnerable, leading to increased reliance on pesticides and synthetic fertilizers. These chemical inputs can wreak havoc on the land, water, and the myriad of organisms that inhabit these spaces. Herein lies another profound advantage of foraging—it eases the strain on commercial agricultural systems. When a segment of the population sources a portion, however small, of their food from the wild, it means that much less land tilled, that many fewer pesticides sprayed, and that much less water used in conventional farming setups. The cascading benefits of this are manifold, ranging from reduced soil erosion to cleaner waterways and healthier pollinator populations.

In essence, sustainable living with foraged foods is more than just a culinary endeavor—it's a profound shift in how we relate to the environment, our food, and ultimately, ourselves. Embracing this lifestyle doesn't just ensure fresher meals on our plates; it's a step towards restoring balance in nature and rekindling a harmonious relationship with the earth.

Foraging as A Spiritual Practice

In the noise and haste of modern life, where nature often fades into the background of urban sprawls and digital screens, foraging emerges not just as a means to procure food, but as a deep spiritual practice. As fingers brush against leaves, as feet tread on earthy trails, and as eyes scour landscapes for hidden treasures, foragers find themselves in an intimate dance with the world around them, awakening senses that urban life might have lulled to sleep. One of the most profound spiritual facets of foraging is the palpable reconnection with nature. Our ancestors were intimately linked to the land, understanding its rhythms, its moods, and its offerings. Over time, as societies moved towards urbanization, this connection became tenuous. Foraging, in its simplicity, reignites this bond. Each venture into the wild is a journey into the heart of the earth, a tactile reminder of the world beyond concrete and glass. There's an unspoken dialogue, a communion, that transpires between the forager and the land. The whispers of the wind, the fragrance of the soil, and the myriad textures of the wild become more than just sensory experiences—they become conduits to understanding our place in the vast web of life.

This deep interaction with nature naturally fosters mindfulness and presence. Unlike supermarket aisles where foods are predictably placed, the wild offers no such assurances. Each foraging expedition demands keen attention, patience, and a heightened sense of awareness. One learns to spot the subtle differences between plants, to listen to the sounds of the forest, to gauge the direction of water sources, and to feel the shifts in weather. In this attentive state, the mind quiets, leaving no room for the incessant chatter of everyday worries. Every step, every glance becomes an exercise in being utterly present. Such mindfulness, often sought in meditation halls, is organically cultivated in the act of foraging.

Hand-in-hand with mindfulness is a profound sense of gratitude and respect. Each edible find is not just a morsel of food; it's a gift from the earth. In recognizing the effort it takes to source food directly from the wild, foragers develop a deep appreciation for every bite they consume. This gratitude extends beyond just the plants or fungi gathered—it envelops the entire ecosystem that nurtures these offerings. The bees that pollinate, the soil microbes that nourish, the rains that hydrate—all play a role in the foraged feast. This understanding instills a profound respect for the environment. Foragers are often at the forefront of conservation efforts, realizing that in protecting the environment, they protect the very source of their sustenance.

A continual journey in foraging is the witnessing of life cycles. Unlike the static imagery of plants we might be accustomed to, foraging introduces one to the dynamic life stages of plants. From the tender shoots of spring to the full bloom of summer, the fruiting in autumn, and the stark dormancy of winter, foragers see the entire spectrum of life played out season after season. This cyclical view offers profound insights into life itself—the growth, the blossoming, the inevitable fading, and the promise of rebirth. It mirrors the ebb and flow of human existence, teaching lessons in impermanence, acceptance, and renewal.

Building Community Through Foraging

Foraging, while often perceived as a solitary pursuit, has roots that run deep in communal collaboration. Historically, gathering was a shared activity, with tribes and communities coming together to seek sustenance from the land. This group effort not only ensured efficiency but became an essential social activity, fostering bonds and ensuring the collective's survival. Today, even in a world where individualism is championed, the act of foraging has retained its potential to knit individuals into tight-knit communities.

At the heart of this communal aspect lies the joy of the shared experience. Venturing out into the wild in groups recreates a setting where ancient stories were spun, knowledge was shared, and memories were crafted. The excitement of a new find, the shared disappointment when searches come up empty, or the collective awe when nature unfolds a spectacle, all become moments of bonding. They bridge generational gaps, with seasoned foragers passing down wisdom to newbies and children, while also weaving a tapestry of shared stories and memories that strengthen communal ties. For those seeking this sense of community, local foraging groups offer a beacon. These groups, often found on social media platforms or community bulletin boards, are a treasure trove of local knowledge and camaraderie. Joining such a group can be an enriching experience, especially for those new to an area or new to the world of foraging. These gatherings become more than just foraging expeditions—they morph into potlucks, swap meets for foraged goods, and a space where lifelong friendships sprout from the shared love of nature.

Further enhancing the community aspect are educational workshops. Such workshops, organized by experienced foragers or local environmental groups, delve deeper into the nuances of foraging. They're spaces where stories are shared, where the wisdom of elders is passed on, where newcomers can learn about local plants, their uses, and preparation methods. Beyond just identification, these workshops often venture into realms like ethical foraging, culinary applications of wild foods, and even the integration of foraged foods into holistic health practices. By organizing or participating in these sessions, individuals not only enrich their knowledge but contribute to a more informed and responsible foraging community. An emerging concept in the world of foraging that beautifully encapsulates the community spirit is Community Supported Foraging (CSF). Borrowing from the ethos of community-supported agriculture, CSF involves communities supporting dedicated foragers, often financially or through other means, who then forage on behalf of the community. The gathered bounty is shared among supporters, ensuring fresh, wild, local produce for all. This model ensures sustainable foraging as the community's vested interest lies in the well-being of the local environment. Moreover, it allows foragers to dedicate more time to their craft, diving deeper into research, and sharing a wider variety of finds with the community.

In weaving together, the act of foraging with community-building, we revisit the age-old wisdom that nature is a binding force, one that draws individuals together in shared purpose and joy. As modern-day foragers step into the wilderness, basket in hand, they're not just seeking food. They're seeking connection, camaraderie, and a sense of belonging in a community that recognizes and celebrates the bounties of the earth.

The Future of Foraging: Challenges and Opportunities

The timeless practice of foraging, a tradition as old as humanity itself, is experiencing a profound resurgence. In a world increasingly distanced from nature by technology and urban sprawl, many are rekindling their ancestral bond with the earth, seeking both sustenance and solace. However, with this renewed interest come challenges that demand introspection and adaptation, even as they open doors to new opportunities.

One of the most pressing concerns as foraging gains popularity is overharvesting. A mushroom patch or a berry bramble, once known only to a few local foragers, can be quickly decimated if shared widely without caution. The sustainability of foraging is its cornerstone; it revolves around the idea that nature offers what she can spare, provided we take only what we need. The rise in the number of foragers demands a collective commitment to ethical practices. Taking only a portion of what's found, allowing plants to complete their life cycle, ensuring regeneration, and understanding the role each plant plays in its ecosystem are foundational to ethical foraging. As the foraging community grows, it bears the responsibility of educating newcomers about these practices to protect the very ecosystems that nourish them.

Legislation and land rights present another labyrinthine challenge. Historically, the act of foraging was a universal right, a means of survival. But in today's world of land ownership and stringent regulations, where one forages can become a legal quagmire. Private lands are obviously off-limits without permission, but even public lands come with their own sets of rules. As foraging gains traction, it's conceivable that future legislation might further regulate it to protect native species or ecosystems. Navigating these rights and potential restrictions will require the foraging community to be informed, respectful, and possibly even engaged in advocacy to ensure access remains open.

In stark contrast to the wilderness, the concrete jungles of our cities are experiencing their own foraging renaissance: urban foraging. City dwellers, yearning for a touch of the wild, are discovering food and medicine in their own backyards. From dandelions in parks to fruit trees in alleys, urban foraging is not only about sustenance but about reconnecting with nature amidst steel and glass. This movement, while exciting, comes with its own challenges, like pollution concerns and land use rights, but underscores the universal desire for natural connection.

Modern technology, often seen as a separator from nature, is playing a pivotal role in this foraging renaissance. Apps equipped with image recognition software can identify plants instantaneously, online communities share knowledge and advice, and GPS can track favorite foraging spots. While they offer significant advantages, there's a cautionary tale here too. Over-reliance can dull the forager's innate skills, and incorrect identifications can lead to harmful consequences.

Our rapidly changing climate casts a shadow of uncertainty on the future of foraging. As temperatures rise and weather patterns become unpredictable, plant distributions shift, and life cycles are disrupted. Foragers might find familiar plants disappearing and new ones taking their place. The onus will be on foragers to continually educate themselves, adapt to these changes, and perhaps even play a role in conserving plants at risk.

Amidst these challenges lie vast opportunities, particularly for entrepreneurship. The world is waking up to the allure of wild, foraged foods. Entrepreneurs can tap into this demand by selling sustainably foraged goods, ensuring they prioritize conservation. Beyond just food, there's a burgeoning market for experiences. Foraging tours, workshops, and retreats are gaining popularity, offering individuals the chance to reconnect with nature under the guidance of seasoned experts.

In conclusion, the future of foraging, while promising, is replete with challenges that demand both respect for tradition and adaptability to change. It's a dance between honoring ancient wisdom and embracing modern realities. As foraging paths meander into the future, they will be shaped by the choices made by today's foragers: choices of sustainability, education, and community. The age-old act of seeking food from the land is evolving, and with mindful steps, it promises a future that's not just about sustenance but about a deeper connection with the earth and each other.

Conclusion

As we close the pages of "Forager's Harvest 101", it's a moment to pause, reflect, and truly assimilate the lessons we've journeyed through together. This book was not just a guide to edible plants, mushrooms, and algae but an invitation into the world of conscious living, of truly seeing, touching, tasting, and understanding the gifts of the Earth. We delved deep into the craft of preservation, ensuring the bounties we collect serve us beyond the moment, allowing us to savor their essence in various culinary masterpieces. These recipes are not just about filling our bellies but filling our souls with the authenticity and freshness of nature's produce. But, more than any practical guide, this book aimed to reconnect you with a forgotten essence — the simple, yet profound joy of sourcing food directly from nature, the way our ancestors did. Our modern lives, so deeply entrenched in technology, often alienate us from the visceral experiences of the world around us. Foraging is a reminder, a reawakening, and a rekindling of that primal bond we share with the Earth. In the shared stories, the communal feasts, the laughter, and the learning, we discover the very essence of humanity. The act of coming together in a world that often pulls us apart is in itself revolutionary. It's a testament to the enduring spirit of community and our inherent need to connect, to belong, to be a part of something greater than ourselves.

For those of you inspired to embark on your own foraging journey, let this book be both a guide and a cautionary tale. The wilderness, while generous, does not forgive ignorance. Approach it with reverence, respect, and the humility of a lifelong learner. Every leaf, every berry, every mushroom holds a story, a lesson. Listen, learn, and always tread with caution. And as we bid adieu, let this be the thought you carry forth: Nature, in its boundless wisdom and generosity, offers us not just sustenance but a path to rediscovery, rejuvenation, and realignment. Embrace it, cherish it, and let it guide you towards a life of abundance, joy, and profound connection. The world is ripe with wonder; all you need to do is step out and savor it.

About The Author

Diane Wells was born into a loving family environment in Florida in 1973. Her father, Jimmy, a lawyer, and her mother, Anna, a teacher of Italian descent, provided her with everything. On many weekends, she relished exploring her paternal grandparents' farm in Georgia, learning about nature and gaining profound experiences. For several years, Diane honed her skills in rhythmic gymnastics, demonstrating great promise. Even then, she faced jealousy and resentment from classmates at school and the gym, who envied her physical prowess, her good looks, and the doting attention she received as an only child. However, Diane's achievements were not merely a result of these advantages. They were built on a foundation of a balanced diet —thanks in large part to her mother's superb Mediterranean cooking— her consistent effort to self-improve, and her resilience against others' judgments, whether positive or negative.

Travel was a significant part of Diane's life, particularly during the summers. Her exposure to different cultures left a lasting impact on her. Guided by these experiences, she pursued a degree in psychology, graduating with honors. She then worked in human resources for a major company before opening her own psychotherapy practice. At 35, Diane married Steve, a business consultant, who shared her passion for travel and exploration. Steve, whom she met while working at her previous company, became the love of her life. Today, they are proud parents of two children, Rebecca and Peter, and share their seaside villa with a beloved Labrador, surrounded by ample greenery.

For the past decade, Diane has consistently practiced Pilates and Yoga to maintain her physical and mental equilibrium, respectively. Despite life's demands, she's never lost touch with her inner child —the girl who once gracefully fluttered on parallel bars and enjoyed nature trips with her grandfather in Georgia. These fond memories inspire her to organize nature walks with her children and friends. Embarking on trails, gathering fruits and plants, and cooking dinner just as her mother taught her, bring immense joy to her life. Her work with people and their problems deepened Diane's understanding of how monotonous routines, poor dietary habits, and insufficient physical activity negatively influence lives.

Now, in her fiftieth year, Diane has chosen to share the secrets of her happiness. Responding to popular demand, she is writing books on the benefits of a simple life, exploring the world, and fostering harmony with life and all living beings.

Made in the USA
Las Vegas, NV
18 March 2024

87416702R00072